Jane —
for the Santa Fe library
Happy Birthday 1985
Michele and Gail

SILVER LINING

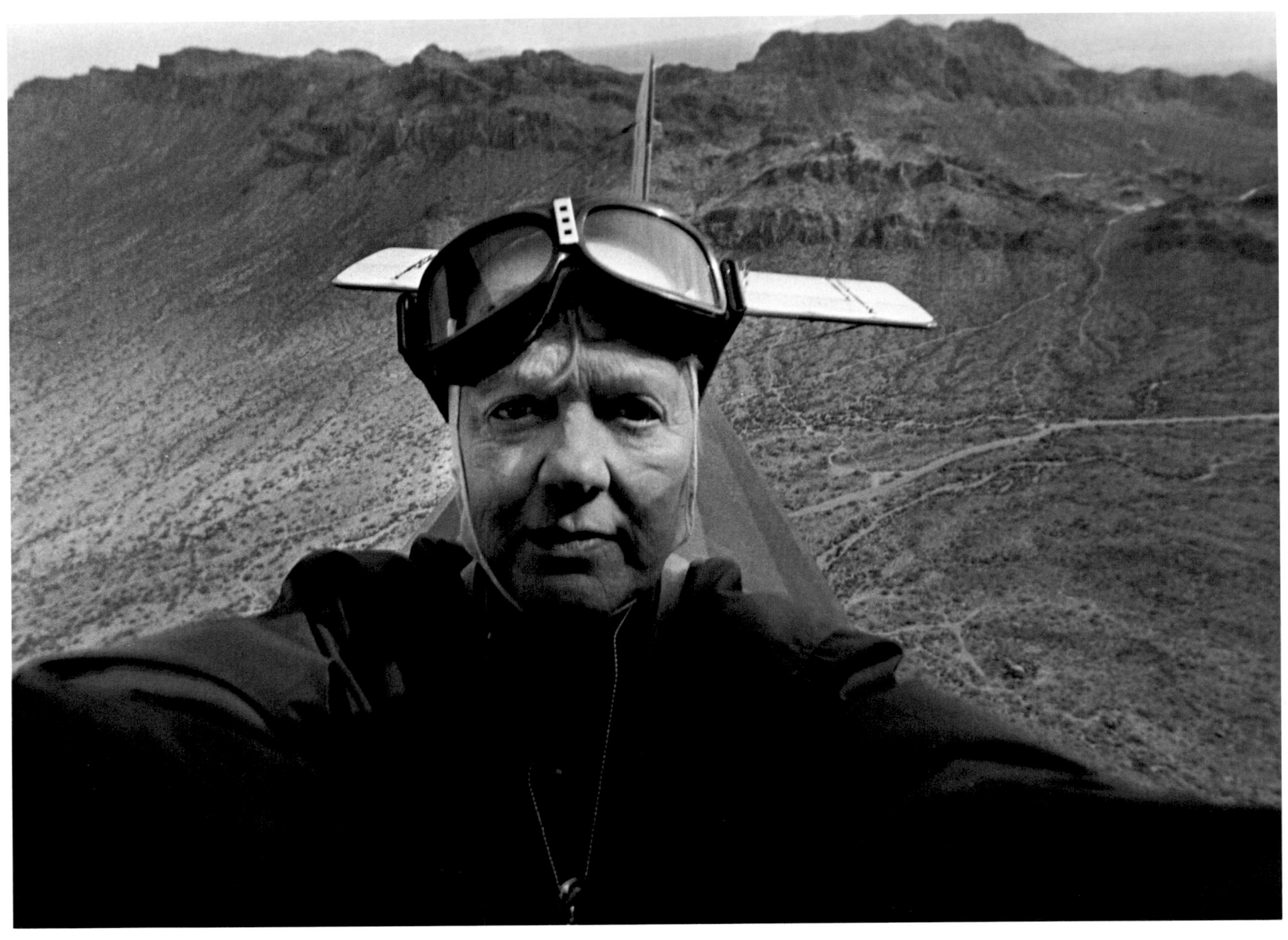

Myself as a Pilot   1982

SILVER LINING
Photographs by Anne Noggle

Text by Janice Zita Grover

Foreword by Van Deren Coke

University of New Mexico Press / Albuquerque

Library of Congress Cataloging in Publication Data

Noggle, Anne, 1922–
   Silver lining.

   1. Photography—Portraits.   2. Noggle, Anne,
1922–   . I. Grover, Janice Zita, 1945–   .
II. Title.
TR680.N63   1983   770′.92′4   83-17072
ISBN 0-8263-0731-0

To Yolanda, Mary, and Shelley,
and to the memory of my mother, Agnes.

My warmest thanks to all the gracious people who have let me take their pictures, and a passing kiss to the photographers who have liked or not liked my work, for they too have had a hand in shaping it.

Special thanks are due to the John Simon Guggenheim Memorial Foundation and the National Endowment for the Arts, whose generous grants allowed me the time and the means to complete work on these photographs. I also wish to thank Sue Gradisar for helping me incorporate into this book some of the ideas originally expressed in the 1983 documentary *Remember Me*.

Contents

Foreword

I first encountered Anne Noggle (*encountered* is the right term, for the word *meet* does not accurately convey the essence of the experience) when I was chairman of the Department of Art at the University of New Mexico. She was an undergraduate art history major taking a course or two each semester. As her adviser, I talked to her at some length about her interesting past and the plans she had for the future. She affected a kind of tough-guy stance, but since she was about my own age I was able to see her as a delightful individual who had firm ideas and a strong vocabulary to express them.

When she had finished her undergraduate study she told me she wanted to leave art history and take a graduate degree in photography. I discouraged her because I felt she had the makings of an insightful art historian. She persisted, however, and finally we agreed that she would work in photography on a trial basis. Within a year she proved that she had an acute eye for faces— for moments when they reflect an emotion or the essence of a personality. Noggle was accepted as a regular graduate student in photography at the University of New Mexico. In the next couple of years she became an accomplished photographer.

She developed a sure grasp of expressive nuances. As a consequence she produces stirring photographs of people one would not ordinarily think of as stirring subjects. Her values are very much her own—she has always been able to see through complacency and pretense. She sees facial furrows as marks people have earned in their lives, which is only fair since she photographs herself with this philosophy in mind. At the same time, her anxieties are those of us all. She throws them into high relief in her photographs of the results of surgery around her eyes after a face-lift.

Noggle is quite blunt about unpleasant realities but does not pander to the tastes of those who like to see people caricatured by the camera. She is not an alien observer like Richard Avedon. She states facts boldly, but she also shows in her pictures how unwarranted is the national psychosis about passing the half-century mark. Her empathy with her subjects is clearly discernible, and it is just as important as her talent as an observer. She is keenly aware that an elderly person may have a jaunty attitude toward life and be capable of much deeper feelings than he or she had when younger. Her subjects may be vain, gloomy, or even neurotic by some people's standards, but they are alive to the fact that their accomplishments have value and meaning.

Some of what she achieves is due to the environment in which she photographs her subjects; their dress and pose give us special insights into their ways of dealing with the world and into their inner tensions. Some of what she achieves, though, has to do with the way she sees beyond just what the camera records. Without the artifice of, say, Arnold Newman, she responds directly to the human spirit. Her pictures convey a sense of intimacy—the intimacy of intense thought. She makes us use our heads and hearts, not just our eyes, when we look at pictures of people.

Without violating the differences between her subjects she has always managed to convey her own vision, though with nuances that differ vastly from picture to picture. In the last five or six years her pictures have begun to fit into an overall pattern; the percentage of really great pictures has increased tremendously. What is consistent and, I do believe, unique about her pictures is their humanism combined with her frankness about aging. These are the things Anne Noggle seems to get down more incisively than the other photographers I can think of.

Van Deren Coke

San Francisco Museum of Modern Art

SILVER LINING

What can I tell you about Anne Noggle's photographs that will not foreclose your own reading of them?

I can tell you something about Anne Noggle herself, at the same time warning you that her photographs cannot be reduced to an equation with her personality or history. I can present the different periods and interests in her work to you, at the same time revealing their underlying and unifying concerns.

I believe that even without an introduction, Noggle's photographs are as clear and large-spirited as any late twentieth-century American portraits can be. At the same time, I believe they are as ambiguous and merciless as any late twentieth-century American portraits can be.

In that paradox lies their power to move us.

—JZG

That time of year thou mayst in me behold
When yellow leaves, or none, or few, do hang
Upon those boughs which shake against the
  cold,
Bare ruin'd choirs, where late the sweet birds
  sang.
In me thou see'st the twilight of such day
As after sunset fadeth in the west;
Which by and by black night doth take away,
Death's second self, that seals up all in rest.
In me thou see'st the glowing of such fire,
That on the ashes of his youth doth lie,
As the death-bed whereon it must expire
Consum'd with that which it was nourish'd by.
  This thou perceiv'st, which makes thy love
    more strong,
  To love that well which thou must leave ere
    long.

Shakespeare, Sonnet LXXIII

Anne Noggle's
Saga of the Fallen Flesh

For the most part, postclassical Western portraiture, whether in painting, sculpture, or photography, has aimed at an optical likeness, in which the portraitist aspires to re-create the physical aspect of the sitter while resisting overt judgment on character, or an ethical likeness, in which the essence of the sitter's moral or social character is suggested. Naturally, portraits can imply a great deal more than individual likenesses alone; we are wont to read an epochal *zeitgeist* into the portraits of practitioners as varied as Holbein, Bronzino, Watteau, Gainsborough, Degas, Dix, Sander, Arbus.

Anne Noggle's portraits may or may not belong in such company; that will be a decision made by our descendants, if such there are. For us, her photographs can be placed more modestly (if also more precisely) within a tradition of photographic portraiture as well as viewed for their documentary value, for they tell us cumulatively something we need to know about their collective subject—aging people.

Noggle's work looks like nobody else's today, yet it owes debts to earlier practitioners in her medium, particularly to Julia Margaret Cameron and August Sander. Noggle came to photography late in life: perhaps it is the press of time that has helped produce so intense and coherent a body of work in less than twenty years. Now, when American art photographers (that is, photographers trained academically and working consciously within or against a tradition of expressive photography) are just beginning after the largely cool and formalist work of the 1970s to reevaluate and reclaim such traditions as portraiture and social documentation, Noggle's work stands out for its already-lengthy and passionate explorations in these areas. In a medium whose most frequent use of the human figure (as in our cultural life as a whole) is to create consumable fantasies, illusions of perpetual youth, Noggle's work stands out for its blunt commitment to the photograph as *memento mori*—the direct evidence of death-in-life.

In viewing Noggle's portraits, we are made aware of how little beyond the superficial indices of age we commonly see in the middle-aged and elderly: the stoop of age, the thinning hair, the startling blue of a still-bright eye against faded skin, the badges of office and authority (the middle-aged man's three-piece business suit, the gloved-and-hatted costume of an elderly lady). But we seldom see—we are not looking for—the gleam of carnality, the self-deprecating humor, the witty maliciousness, the sensuality, for these are qualities we have appropriated and redistributed exclusively among the young.

Noggle sees these traits in age; she tricks them out of her subjects. She treats age with irreverence, acidity, respect, humor, melancholy—a myriad of ways, none of them what we might conventionally expect. And her subjects respond in equally various and unanticipated ways: with seductiveness (*Ruth Leakey,* 1980), girlishness (*Edith "Tiny" Keene,* 1981), coquetry (*N. B.,* 1982), droll humor (*Yolanda in the Patio,* 1981). Noggle also stares hard at the evidence that age isolates as it kills (*Agnes,* 1978).

How did Anne Noggle come to make such a distinctive and revelatory body of work? The traceable part of the answer lies, I think, in the peculiar circumstances of her personal experience. I don't say this lightly, since it is obvious that everyone's personal experience goes into the making of her or his art. Nor do I wish to appear to suggest a kind of biographical determinism, though this is a rhetorical strategy that Noggle herself will sometimes fall back on in speaking of her own work: "I want and still want to photograph what moves me. It is akin to poetry in that you have no choice of what you do. It is whatever is inside that demands to be seen." At the risk of being tendentious, though, I will say that the facts of Noggle's several wholly separate careers—as a flyer and as a military officer, as an artist beginning a career only in middle age—seem to have played decisive roles in empowering her to do the particular work she has chosen.

Noggle was born in Evanston, Illinois, in 1922. She was raised among women: her mother supported her two daughters by managing a bookstore in Chicago's Loop, and the three of them lived together in a boarding house from which Anne, the younger and dreamier daughter, spun out fantasies of

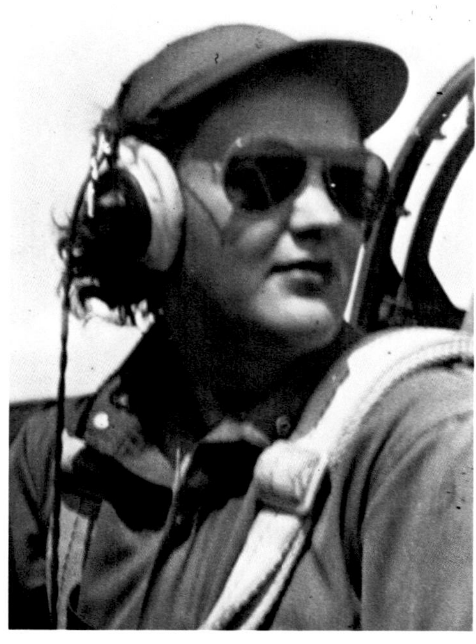

Anne Noggle, 1943

flying. By her senior year in high school, those fantasies were tentative realities: Noggle won her student license in 1940, at a time when there were few women pilots in the United States. For a young girl with no financial resources, the barriers to flight were almost overwhelming. Yet Noggle overcame them, becoming not only a pilot, but a flight instructor as a Women's Air Force Service Pilot (WASP) during World War II.

Following the War, Noggle taught flying, joined an aerial circus doing stunt flying, and later crop-dusted throughout the Southwest. "We never thought about the future," she recalls.

> We made a hundred dollars or so in a few hours a day and spent it all every night drinking and carousing. The statistics were that the average crop-duster pilot had a life-span of about a year and a half. You lived on a high that danger bestows on you. Only *now* counted.
>
> Everyday details just didn't count. I used to buy socks and when they were soiled, I just tossed them in the wastebasket and

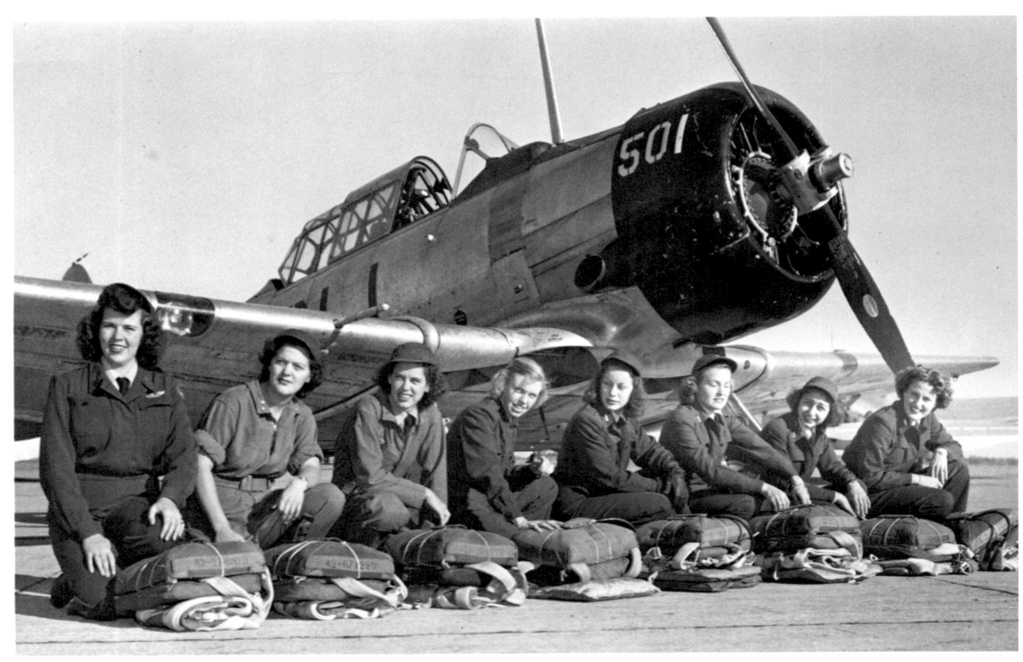

Anne Noggle as a WASP

bought new ones. One evening my landlady in some Texas town
presented me with this mound of socks that she had salvaged
from the trash and washed for me. She said it was terrible the
way I threw away new, perfectly good socks. But that's how we
all lived . . .

Noggle's devil-may-care living ended with her decision to go on active
duty with the Air Force and get overseas. She was assigned as an intercept-
controller and later served in Paris as a protocol officer. It was there that her
interest in art began: when she wasn't on duty, she wandered Paris and
discovered the Louvre. After that, she spent much of her spare time there.

An early and forced disability retirement due to emphysema caused by
crop-dusting brought Noggle to New Mexico, where her mother and older
sister now lived. Noggle decided to enter the University of New Mexico in
1959 as a thirty-eight-year-old freshman majoring in art history. In her first
photography class (taken reluctantly as part of a studio requirement), the
power of photography metaphorically swam up at her out of the developing

8

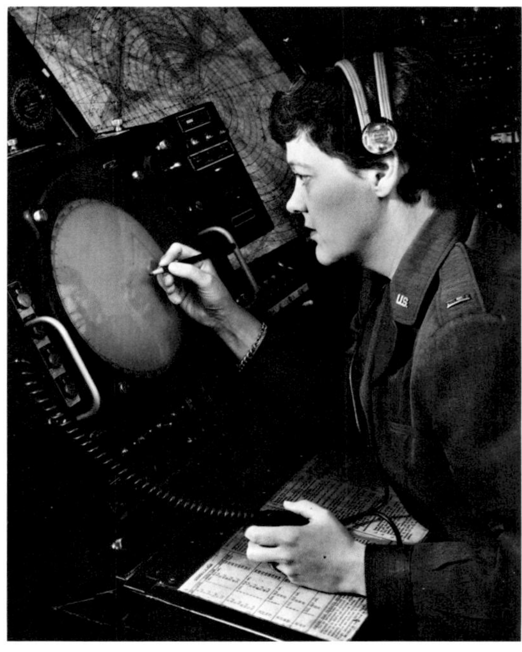

Anne Noggle as an intercept-controller

tray. As she saw her first print emerging, Noggle recalls, "It was the first time since I'd been grounded that I felt the same excitement that flying always gave me. I was purely and completely happy. Now I knew what I was going to do for the rest of my life."

The two careers, linked initially only by the emotion they elicited ("As a romantic, I think intent is subservient to expression"), seemed to her later to be similar in other ways as well:

> Flying is for the young to do and the middle-aged to dream
> about. There is a resemblance, I think, between flying and
> photography. Both are done alone in concept anyway, and both
> require independence and optimism and some dumb courage.

Noggle needed to fall back on these qualities to sustain her work for the first decade. The late 1960s, when she began to photograph seriously, was not a period—either at the University of New Mexico or in American academic photography circles generally—that provided much support for the subject and approach that attracted Noggle. The climate within the Art Department faculty was cool and process-oriented and indifferent to portraiture. As Noggle recalls it,

> I was too young in photography and we were too isolated [in
> Albuquerque] to know what was really happening around the
> country, and we (Cavalliere Ketchum and Jim Alinder and others)
> went our own way and were supported equally by Coke.

Van Deren Coke shaped the photography program at the University of New Mexico, first as the Art Department's chairman and later as director of the Art Museum. Though consistently supportive of Noggle's work, Coke's professional bias—and, in turn, that of the department he created—came to favor photographers like Heinecken and Fichter whose formalist concerns and painterly/print-maker's approaches to photography were linked to nonphotographic art movements. Noggle's portraits were minority reports from what was at that time a minority genre. Fortunately, she "never considered success or failure."

> I had to photograph what I wanted to photograph and I simply
> moved in my own direction and paid no attention to what went
> on around me. Even that early on, I knew where I was and I
> knew that by looking back at my work, I could realize where I
> was going by where I came from. Sophocles said something like,
> "We have to wait till sunset to see how beautiful the day has
> been," and I didn't want to compete. I never have liked
> competition and stayed away from it.

Noggle's earliest successes—images that corresponded to her own romantic intuition about their "rightness"—were long, narrow 140° photographs made with a 35mm Panon camera. In most of them, the photograph takes in a middle-aged or elderly sitter and her surroundings. It is characteristic of the wide-field lens to distort space in such a way that subjects distant from the lens appear flattened against deep space; between this effect and the necessity for reading the image side to side, the format gets as close as the still camera can to the implied narrative unfolding of a panoramic opening shot in a film. It suggests distance between seer and seen; it conflates sitter and setting. Noggle's Panon images of her mother's circle in Santa Fe have exactly these qualities, as if a newly landed observer (as in a sense Noggle, reborn as a photographer, was) were scrutinizing these women, their curious rites and settings, for the first time.

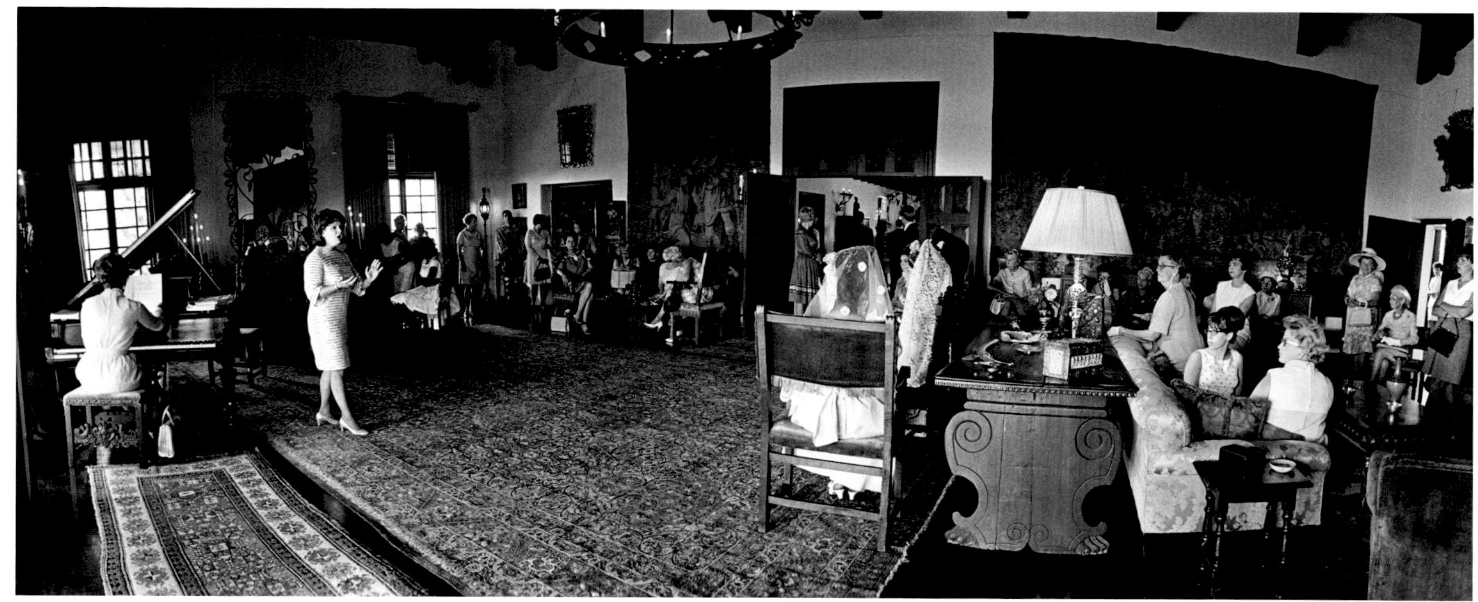

The Recital   1969

It was at this point that Noggle, along with many of her fellow-students, discovered Diane Arbus's work, which became an important influence. Like many artists', Noggle's reading of art and photographic history is essentially intuitive and appropriative: she views to learn others' strategies, to feed her own creativity. Arbus, she says,

> freed all of us to do as we pleased with our subjects if we wanted
> to do that. Before I saw Arbus's work, if I saw something—a
> piece of crumpled paper, for instance, in front of my subject—I'd
> either move myself, the camera, or my subject, or I'd kick the
> paper out of the way, but after looking at Arbus, I knew I didn't
> have to do that anymore.

Before looking at Arbus's work, Noggle had worked within the influence of an older, documentary tradition typified by Cartier-Bresson: "I thought he was really exceptional. He didn't touch or change anything but just waited for the picture to fall into place." Arbus's mannered use of the revealing clutter of ordinary lives, I would argue, became an equally important part of the strategy of Noggle's work—not as a stylistic homage to Arbus, but as a device proven both visually and metaphorically in another's powerful body of work.

Noggle's debt to Arbus didn't end there. She submitted some of her early work to an exhibition juried by Arbus as part the Pennsylvania Festival of the Arts and received the kind of confirmation of her own intuitions that she needed:

> The prize was $100 cash, and I was sure that I would win it—
> just positive. Eight or ten weeks went by, but no word. Finally
> the prints themselves came back, but there was no letter or
> anything with them, no cash. But I *still* knew that I'd won, and
> sure enough, about two weeks later a letter came with the check
> for $100. *She'd liked them.*

Noggle also discovered the work of Julia Margaret Cameron: "I knew immediately that she and I were kindred spirits, for her people are alive today, and they vibrate that aliveness—the past is not dead, it has just already happened."

There was a substantial parallel between what Noggle was trying to achieve in her work and Cameron's portraits. Just as Noggle undertook portraiture in a period that valued other photographic enterprises more highly, so Cameron wished, in the midst of a positivist era that believed in a physiognomic approach to depiction, to make expressive portraits. Rather than depicting the surface, Cameron wished to reveal the moral essence of her sitters, and she used unorthodox means to achieve this goal:

> When I have such men {as Thomas Carlyle} before my camera my
> whole soul has endeavoured to do its duty towards them in
> recording faithfully the greatness of the inner as well as the
> features of the outer man.[1]

Thus Cameron's technically irregular effects were, for her, not lapses in skill but instead means to an end that transcended mere optical realism:

> my first successes in my out-of-focus pictures were a fluke. That
> is to say, that when focussing and coming to something which,

---

1. Cameron, "The Annals of My Glass House" (1974), rept. in Beaumont Newhall, ed., *Photography: Essays and Images* (New York: Museum of Modern Art, 1980), p. 137.

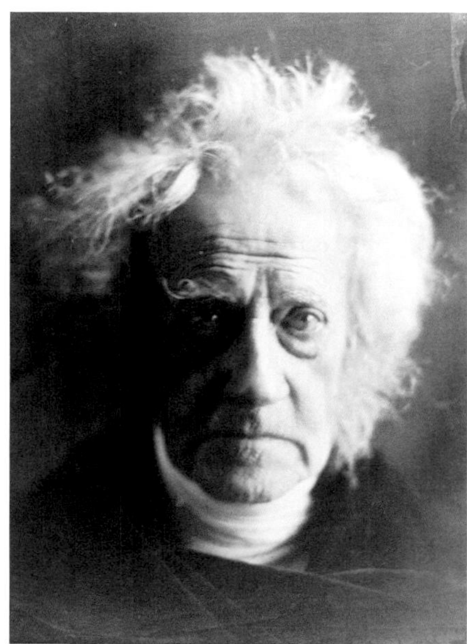

Julia Margaret Cameron, *Sir John Herschel,* 1867. Courtesy Gernsheim Collection, Humanities Research Center, the University of Texas at Austin.

to my eye, was very beautiful, I stopped there instead of screwing
on the lens to the more definite focus which all other
photographers insist upon.[2]

It is Cameron's romantic insistence on the primacy of feeling and the subordination of technique to effect that Noggle has taken from her reading of Cameron's work. These lessons are as visible in a photograph like *Morris* (1976), in which the forced perspective of an extreme wide-angle lens renders cat far larger than owner, as they are in photographs more directly related to Cameron, like *Agnes in a Fur Collar* (1979), in which the dramatic chiaroscuro and shallow depth of field are used to suggest character in a manner reminiscent of Cameron's *Sir John Herschel* (1867).

---

2. Ibid., p. 136. *All other photographers* is, of course, an exaggeration: Cameron's use of out-of-focus and soft focus effects were common, if hotly debated, in mid-nineteenth-century English photography circles.

The artist's life, whatever the medium, whatever the accomplishment, never becomes easier on a day-to-day basis. While the odds of more frequent or continued success may increase, there's little comfort in this knowledge: the possibility of failure *right now, this time,* seems as great as ever. To cut off comforting everyday contacts, the sort of human transactions that are prompted by unqualified affection rather than by superior performance, to voluntarily court opportunities for seeing how signally one can fail, to close one's life into an intense solitude requires great discipline and courage.

It is a discipline that Noggle had already learned and applied to exacting fields before photography, but this time it was turned wholly inward: no airplane or duty-roster defined the apportioning of her time or the accomplishment of her goals.

But Noggle enjoys risks. In fact, the impetus for all three of her careers, it could plausibly be argued, was a need to test herself against unknowns, to move beyond convention, to burn her bridges behind her. In her inversion of private and public faces (the face-lift series), in the very act of making portraits to please herself rather than the sitter, she courts social and personal risks, at the same time priding herself on the transparency of her motives and ambition: "I thought I would make myself transparent in a Walter Mitty–like way . . . the self as hero and protagonist."

Noggle came out of the service into a world of the very young—the university, where her fellow students were twenty years younger than she. Her mother's circle, where she photographed, was some twenty-five years older than she. Out of these sharp contrasts and her own aging grew the focus of her photographic inquiry:

> I have something that I want to show and it concerns the way it
> is to *be,* and the way it is to see yourself and those around you as
> you have become. Change is the big surprise in its aspects, how
> it affects you, how you cope and sometimes how you don't cope.
> It is a very visual thing and the first time that how I *look* has
> affected how I *feel* about myself.

After 1970, Noggle began to photograph herself and her acquaintances at closer range. The Panon images gave way in the early 1970s to wide-angle 35mm portraits of her mother, Agnes; Agnes's friend Yolanda; Anne's sister, Mary; and assorted other friends and relations. Rather like a polished repertory company, this small cast of characters appears and reappears in Noggle's work over the course of two decades, and we are fascinated and saddened to see the changes written on them as age overtakes them ("I photograph the saga of the fallen flesh," Noggle explains).

Noggle depended in this work not on the formally provocative properties of the elongated Panon format but rather on a quirky sense of timing and framing that made seemingly routine moments appear unsettling or portentous. Most of Noggle's successful early and mid 1970s images owe their strength to her knowledge of her subjects and her ability to translate that knowledge into visual terms: knowing the characteristic gesture or expression that could stand metonymously for her subject's character or emotion, Noggle would wait for the appropriate moment and make her exposure.

The images came slowly in the early 1970s. Much of Noggle's time then was given over to curatorial work. Besides acting as photographic curator to the Museum of Fine Arts in Santa Fe, she and the late Margery Mann guest-curated a large (250 prints) exhibition, "Women of Photography: An Historical Survey," at the San Francisco Museum of Modern Art in 1975. That spring, she was informed that she had been awarded a National Endowment for the Arts photographer's grant.

The project Noggle proposed spending her first NEA grant on (she received a second grant in 1978) would take her back and forth across the country, photographing older women.

> I thought then that environment was definitive and proposed
> photographing older women in their own homes because they
> would have an accumulation of belongings and memorabilia that
> would tell us about them and our culture.

This first attempt in 1975–76 to break into a wider world of subjects was not a success in Noggle's view; few of the photographs from this period seemed expressively right to her, and those few that did were "too easy"—their visual strangeness a product of formal means (e.g., *La Jolla No. 3,* 1975) rather than of a conjoining of intellectual and emotional "rightness." Her frustration with documenting unknown lives led her to repudiate not only the work but also the values and methods she had brought to the project—a documentarian's detachment and seemingly transparent technique. She rejected these in favor of their opposites—a far looser, riskier technique, one which courted chance, and a conviction that she would have to provoke the realities she sought rather than merely record existing ones. Noggle's own recognition of this change in what she sought came slowly at first:

> During this period [the NEA year] I was taking photographs that I rejected intellectually, for they didn't have a place in the concept of what I had set out to do. These images led to the burst of activity that took place in late 1975 and 1976. These were images that I had suppressed earlier in '75. The big shock was that I had *changed* and had difficulty accepting that, as I thought that when you grew up and decided what you wanted to photograph, then you just did that and hoped you would get better at it.

> But the change really was a change in attitude from recording what was *there* to actively creating photographs. . . . Now I know that we do change all our lives or calcify.

Some of the first striking work emerging from this emotionally riskier attitude was Noggle's face-lift series (1975), in which she turned her eye on herself with the same half-loving, half-cruel curiosity that she employed in photographing others. From the last self-portrait preceding the operation—an unsparing, pore-close scrutiny in harsh midday sunlight—to the postoperative healing, Noggle recorded the physical changes:

> For someone who's so interested in aging, it's hard for me to explain about my face-lift . . . I've always been fascinated by something about my face, and it's interesting to see the changes and reverse them but at the same time see that they're taking place anyway . . . If I am shown in my face-lift as attempting to stave off the visible aging process, it is also an indication of what an exercise in futility that is.

Noggle worked in closer in these self-portraits than she had been accustomed to with other subjects, and it is a combination of this insistently intimate, confrontational closeness and the taboo subject matter that gives the images their power. (They also redeem somewhat the mordancy of her portraits of others, for we can see that she is no more willing to spare herself than she is her other subjects.) Like her hero, Julia Margaret Cameron, Noggle succeeded here in wedding a detailed physical scrutiny with an expressive

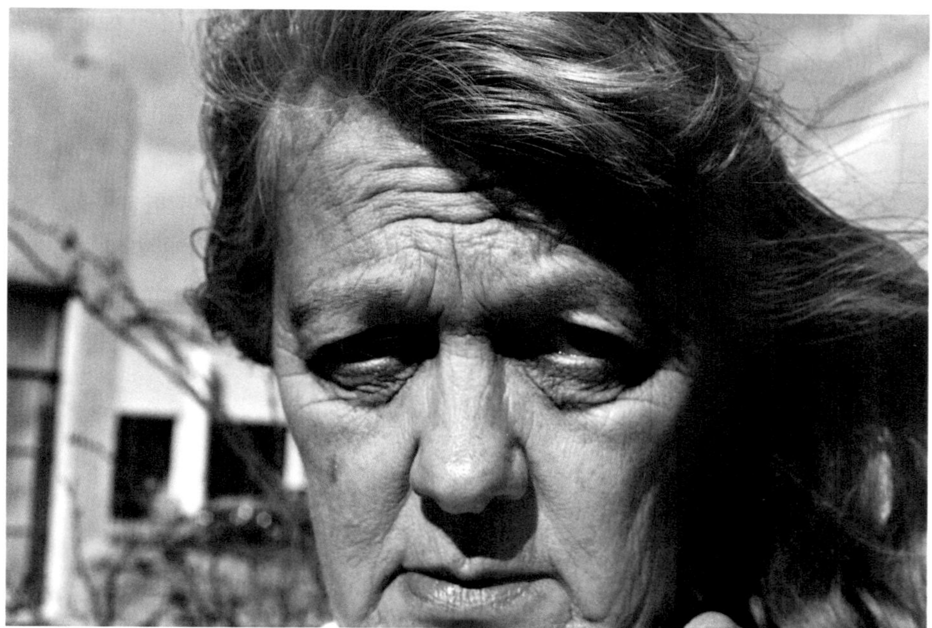

Self-portrait Before Surgery   1975

depiction of character. Both tough and wistful, Noggle's bruised face stares out at the camera/herself/us, the toughness belied by the romantic, drooping rose between her swollen lips and the toy plane in the background, a symbol of Noggle's various forced groundings (Face-lift No. 3).

When these photographs were first exhibited in 1976, they caused a flurry of excitement among viewers, a reaction not at all common in art photography's usually decorous precincts. The reaction, though not on the scale of viewer response to Arbus's work (Noggle has never been so widely known), was similar in the manner in which viewers connected the images to their antecedents in life.

Unlike the formally preoccupied work of so many 1970s art photographers, Noggle's images pulled the viewer back toward life, armed, one might say, with new visions of what aging and portraiture might mean. Middle-aged women who were contemplating face-lifts or had had them, younger women peering anxiously ahead, men interested in the parts beauty and aging played in women's lives wrote to Noggle, approached her at conferences, lectures, and galleries, and told her that her face-lift portraits had meant something to them. The photographs and their maker became a sort of early-warning system to those who saw them.

Characteristically, Noggle depreciates the series now and says she is "sick of it"—like most artists and photographers known for a particular body of work, she feels constrained by its celebrity and eager to move beyond it. But the work was important at the time because

> it was like opening up the gates and the new images poured out.
> I was taken aback by the amount of intensity of the new work,
> not at all cool and documentary, but instead messages from
> within. *I was moving from outside myself to inside myself.* I felt it so
> strongly and I immediately knew that I was now right in the
> middle of me and images were suddenly everywhere—a fecundity
> of them. It was wonderful and I loved them and didn't give a
> damn if anyone else did or not.

The face-lift series was also the start of a strong, large body of self-portraits, work that more than any other has attracted the attention of Noggle's fellow photographers and curators. Pressure to exhibit her self-portraits as a group exists (as it did during the making of this book), but Noggle resists the idea:

> the self-portraits and portraits need not be separated, for they
> spring from the same source . . . they're more closely related to
> what I'm doing with other portraits at a given time than they are
> to each other.

Nevertheless, it seems true that in her work, the principal shifts in approach can be seen first and sometimes with greatest clarity in the self-portraits. If this is so, perhaps it is because

> I use myself at times as a model to express something (usually to
> do with the way time shapes and changes us) that I think in a
> way other people would be reluctant to be pictured . . . perhaps
> I am more spontaneous in self-images. That is when the camera is
> *alter ego,* not deliberate, but impulsive.

Following the 1975 face-lift series, Noggle returned to the subjects she knew best—her friends and family. She no longer limited herself to close observations of familiar faces, no longer waited hunter-like to capture the essence of familiar character: instead, she *created* plausible illusions, manufactured realities, spun tales that might or might not have anything reliable to do with her cast of characters. This work, which is some of her strongest to date, extends from 1976 through 1980. The bulk of it falls into three categories: portraits of her usual cast of largely female sitters, the portraits of Agnes, and the *Silver Lining* series of portraits of middle-aged and elderly couples.

Again, a self-portrait (1976) stands as a sort of benchmark of the elements that would appear in the other photographs of herself, of Shelley, and of Yolanda: Noggle driving as she photographs, a long hand-held exposure mated to a strobe so that her face appears at once as a plasm of movement and a hard-edged profile set against the curiously artificial brightness of the flash-filled car.[3] Speed, the discipline of driving, the anonymity and freedom of the desert highway, the pure risk of photographing under such conditions appear to be peculiarly conducive to Noggle's inner eye ("I know how I will look by how I feel"), for she looks very different in self-portraits taken while driving from the way she looks in her stationary studies—she takes more chances with expression, gesture, framing. Unlike her "grounded" self-portraits, which have all the blunt finality and heaviness of funeral portraits, these images appear fluid, even playful.

So does the work that surrounds this self-portrait. During the same period, Noggle was experimenting with long exposure times that recorded subject movement, ambient light, and camera shake as well as with short spurts of strobe light that illuminated her principal subject but fell off sharply behind and around it. *Shelley* (1978) is paradigmatic of Noggle's use of these techniques.

Shelley positions its principal subject off-center in the harsh glare of flash; beneath its hard-edged glare, the flesh and hair seem about to melt, to lose definition. Behind Shelley, the figure of a young man runs toward her, as out of a nightmare, for he is faceless, his features almost wholly obscured by the fall-off strobe lights. Only the stripes of his jersey, his clenched fist and powerful right arm are clearly visible. Behind him, a stormy sky and a tangle of power lines close the two figures into a disquieting relationship. Here, age

---

3. Photographing while driving is endemic in the Southwest, where long distances and monotonous landscapes make the self an appealing subject even to nonportraitists. In Noggle's own work, there are several notably successful self-portraits made in the car, *i.e., Self-image* (1979), *Southwest Passage* (1982), *Myself as Guggenheim Fellow* (1982).

is personified and youth is not. Age/femaleness looks vulnerable and youth/maleness appears as an anonymous aggressor.

A number of Noggle's finest self-portraits were made in the period 1975–80. *Myself, 7 A.M.* (1977), *Self-image in Cochiti Lake* (1977), *Stonehenge Decoded* (1977), *Self-image No. 2* (1978), and *Reminiscence: Portrait with My Sister* (1980) chronicle the changes in Noggle's body, symbolized here by a mortal shadow falling across the body (*Myself, 7A.M.*), death-by-drowning (*Self-image in Cochiti Lake*, in which Noggle appears floating in opaque water, a be-pearled and made-up middle-aged Ophelia), and the equation of the sere and ancient New Mexico landscape with her own torso (*Self-image No. 2* and *Stonehenge Decoded*).

During this period, Noggle also completed a harrowing series of portraits of her mother, Agnes, as this proud spirit succumbed to her final illness. What started out in 1970 as documentation-from-a-distance of a handsome, imperious-looking woman seated in a spacious restaurant (*La Posada,* 1970) devolves into the image of a dried stick of a figure, fierce-eyed and dwarfed even by her small cluttered room, taken shortly before Agnes's death (*Agnes,* 1979). In between, Noggle's portraits of Agnes were made at close range: direct and simple confrontations between the subject and the photographer. *Agnes* (1976) shows us the decay implicit in the first image: now age is burned into its subject. Gaunt and distorted, both by a glass shower-door and by age, Agnes stares out at us from eyes so shadowed by age's pull that she could as easily be an old man as an old woman. Above her, a plastic bag hangs suspended, the ever-new and imperishable, the inorganic. A scythe-like etching on the frosted shower-door seems to embed itself in Agnes's left temple like a mortal sentence. One needn't know that Agnes's death was imminent to recognize its symbolic presence.

The sea-changes in another of Noggle's intimates are charted in *Santa Fe Spring* (1976), *Santa Fe Summer No. 1* (1976), *Yolanda in Her Silk Hat* (1980), *Yolanda, Veiled Image* (1980), *Yolanda in the Patio* (1981), and *Yolanda* (1983). The first two of these images use the techniques common to Noggle's 1976–78 work (*e.g., Shelley, Hot Flash*); thereafter, Noggle's camera moves closer and closer to its subject, as if the secrets of aging might be found in the lines of her face. By turns somber, mischievous, abstracted, Yolanda defies categorization. The photographs capture facial expressions and gestures which suggest that old age is a foreign land, one in which the familiar landmarks of human expression point to new meanings. One comes away from viewing

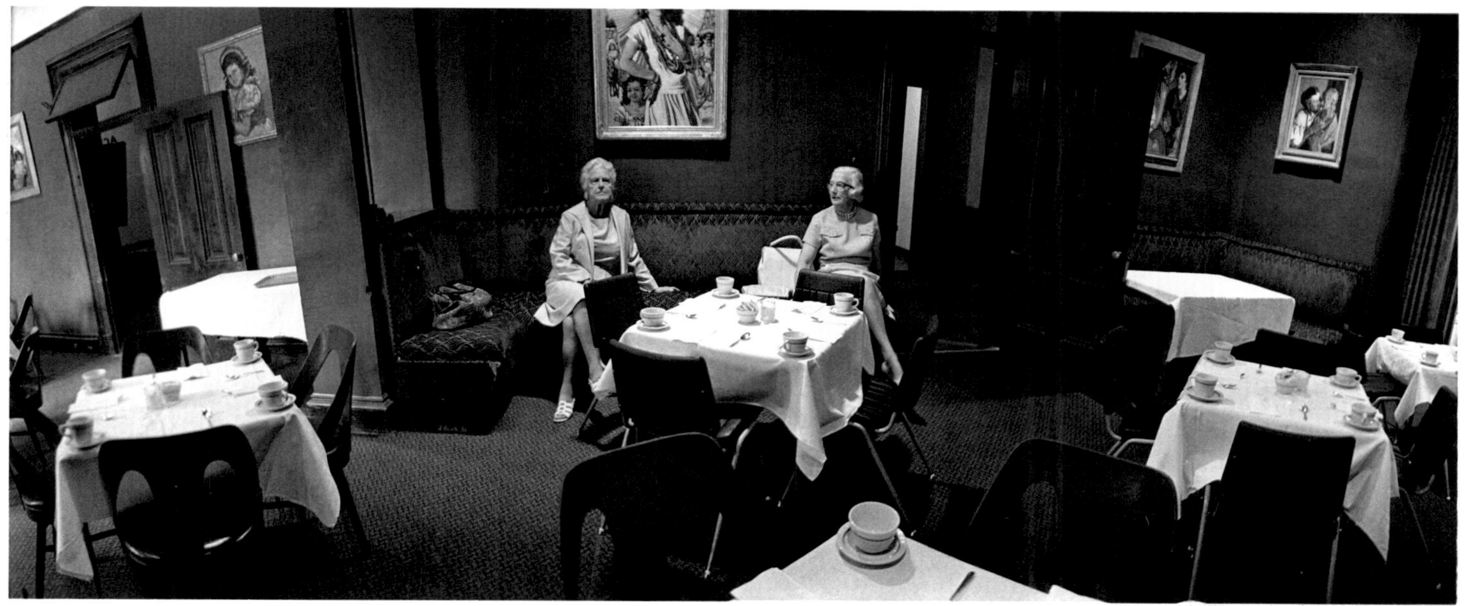

La Posada   1970

this extended portrait with contradictory views of its subject, which is very much to Noggle's point: the human personality, even under the stress and fray of aging, still expands and flows, still is capable of change and surprise.

In 1978, Noggle undertook a series she called *Silver Lining,* portraits of married couples. Previous to this series, men had made only fitful appearances in Noggle's work. Here, their relationships to their mates appear, if not peripheral, at least subordinate: the women are placed either closer (and hence in more intimate relationship) to us or respond more expressively to the camera's gaze.

One would like to have been a fly on the wall during one of these portrait sessions. The images are unencumbered by the fanciful techniques or quirky timing of other portraits during this period, and the stiff, sometimes stagey postures of the subjects seems to suggest that the sitters played a large part in determining their own settings, costumes, and poses. Noggle has commented that the actual strength/weakness of the sitters in these dual portraits was sometimes the reverse of that pictured, but as an explanation, this only furthers their mystery. To my eye, the marked differences in expression of the men and women, combined with the physical ascendancy of the latter, creates a sense of estrangement within the relationships. That this is so can be adduced by comparing these portraits with those that Noggle made in Seattle in 1982, in which couples not only stand closer together and respond to the camera in similar ways but also look alike, their individual differences smoothed by the passage of shared time. *Silver Lining*'s formal strategies seem to imply a more pessimistic (or at any rate, more ambiguous) view of marriage:

> *Silver Lining* is supposed to have as its basis that irony implicit in
> living together for so long—a double-edged idea that life
> together is and isn't a bowl of cherries—and trying to indicate it
> by not giving the answer in the images. I love the enigma of it
> all.

The series continues to hold Noggle's own affection, for it hangs in her home like a gallery of timeless reflections on a road-not-taken by the photographer herself.

In 1981, Noggle began again to explore a way of making portraits that she had attempted and failed at during her first NEA grant. Her closed circle of subjects had become too restrictive: "I got tired of trying to do stripped-down portraits where I was drawing out someone's essence—I wanted to photograph the surface."

A National Endowment for the Arts grant for a New Mexico photographic survey hastened the change. Noggle's part in the grant would be to photograph New Mexicans in Albuquerque and Santa Fe, and she realized that the project was the appropriate vehicle for the change she was contemplating. Before the survey, Noggle's working method had involved a great deal of preplanning; she would

> lie awake at night and try out different ways of photographing a
> person. It was a sort of visual sorting—picturing them in
> different spaces doing various things, deciding whether an image
> would work or not—this creating images in my mind, playing
> around with them, improvising, went on all the time. I even

woke up in the night and found myself thinking about it in my
sleep.

About the time the survey project was funded, Noggle acquired a new
and far more complete text from Germany on August Sander's work. Sander's
anatomy of Weimar society sparked Noggle's wish to photograph in an equally
dispassionate way, though not without misgiving:

> I was apprehensive about the change but decided to commit
> myself to it and to accept the idea that a whole body of work
> could be more than the sum of its parts. The work would be
> much lower-keyed than my old way of working, where I expected
> each image to be able to stand alone or else I discarded it.

Most of Noggle's survey subjects, as well as those she photographed in
Texas and Seattle on her 1982 Guggenheim fellowship, were people she had
never seen before and knew little about. The new portraits depended upon
split-second decisions about lighting, setting, pose, and expression. They
were more frontal, more static; the stylistic influence of Sander was evident
in the centering of subjects, the respectful, documentary distance at which
they were frequently photographed, the quantity of information about surroundings, clothing, possessions. Noggle returned to the use of natural light
and unobtrusive flash. It is as if all of her earlier experiments, lessons, seeing
found a place in these low-key portraits—the telling details she saw in Arbus's
work and sought in her own 1975 NEA work, the expressive language of
gesture and technique she loved in Cameron, the eye for humor and grit she
had developed in herself. Perhaps most important, she worked to quell an
urge to impose her own will on her subjects, ending by accepting them as
they are:

> There was one woman in Seattle, 42 or 43, beautiful, with dark
> hair—she looked sort of like Loretta Young, and she was so
> beautiful, and her face was *so empty,* that I decided I couldn't use
> her photograph, but now I've decided to reprint it. Her surface is
> just blank, but *that's* real, too.
>
> When I went to photograph her, I wanted her standing in a
> door, and while I walked out to where I was going to stand, she
> posed herself in the doorway with one foot slightly behind the
> other, arms out to hold the door jamb, with her shawl draped

just so—very lady-like and studied. And I said, *"No, no,* not like
that!" And I was *so wrong*—that was just as real as something un-
self-conscious. Because she didn't have an un-self-conscious bone
in her body, after all.

In these *Seattle Faces* (1982) and the Texas portraits that followed, Noggle
has managed to apply the strengths she found in Sander's work to her own
concerns for aging—a seeming transparency of attitude on the photographer's
part that leaves viewers feeling that they are seeing only the subject and not
the photographer's partial view of the subject. No idiosyncrasies of framing,
lighting, or pose are evident here. There are no interrupted gestures or transient
expressions to mediate the illusion these portraits create. Instead, they seem
final in their formality, their sense of a measured and conscious presentation
of self to the camera. *This is how we wish to look,* most of the subjects seem
to say.

Yet that something in Noggle's gaze that seeks out the signs of mortality
overlays the self-presentation like a transparent glaze. Subjects' aging bodies
take on a visual importance equivalent to but distinct from their projected
character—hands (*H. M. W., K. B.*), the tug of gravity on the flesh of faces
(*A. P., V. P.*), the likenesses between man and woman that age and lengthy
relationships imprint (*A. R. and D. R., B. A. and W. A.*).

One senses Noggle's own deeply conflicting responses to aging in these
portraits. For while the subjects are invariably treated respectfully, they are
offered no quarter in the ways that commercial portraiture, for example,
accommodates aging—by softening focus and lighting on women or by em-
phasizing the rough texture of male skin with strong side-lighting. Noggle's
portraits insist that our appearance tells our story best without these artifices—
and creates a new set of them instead.

For no matter how natural Noggle's portraits may appear, they are as
wholly a matter of her particular vision of things as a commercial portrait or
an Arbus portrait is a record of these very different social visions. In Noggle's
work, age is the impersonal catalyst of character, and she documents its
encroachments sedulously, watches as it gradually displaces personality with
death.

From the standpoint of ordinary human life things appear in a
natural order, a definite hierarchy. . . . It is enough to upset the

value pattern and to produce an art in which the small events of
life appear in the foreground with monumental dimensions.

—José Ortega y Gasset,
The Dehumanization of Art (1925)

Noggle's intention, insofar as she announces it outside the work itself,
is to reveal the spirit in her sitters and to capture changes that come over the
human countenance as it ages. She wants her photographs, she says, "to be
alive forever." At the deepest level, this urge to make images proceeds out of
her own need to control death through her work, to overcome it:

> I could tell you all about the changes the body goes through at
> forty, fifty, sixty. Sometimes I'll lie in bed at night and hold up
> my arm and stare at the way the skin falls away from it and I'll
> think, *"Hmmmm."* First the upper arm thickens and then the flesh
> sort of falls away from the arms, and then the flesh falls down
> from the upper leg and produces these bags over the knees, and
> then it does the same thing lower down, around the ankles. I say
> it's gravity seeking gravity, the something in us that wants to
> die.

The faces and bodies looking out of Noggle's self-portraits and portraits
are full of self-knowledge (if not always self-acceptance), reminding us of
Orwell's adage, "At 50, everyone has the face he deserves." But what seems
most striking about these faces is their openness and ease before Noggle, which
lets us see their range of responses. They are not forced into a stylistic or
substantive procrustean bed, but rather demonstrate a variety of reactions to
the opportunity of presenting themselves to the scrutiny of another human
being with a camera.

If we compare these portraits to those of middle-aged and elderly women
in Diane Arbus's work,[4] the breadth and generosity of Noggle's achievement

---

4. E.g., *Elderly Couple on a Park Bench, N.Y.C. 1969, Burlesque Comedienne in Her Dressing Room, Atlantic City, N.J., 1963, A Woman with Pearl Necklace and Earrings, N.Y.C., 1967, Woman on a Park Bench on a Sunny Day, N.Y.C. 1969, The King and Queen of a Senior Citizens Dance, N.Y.C. 1970, A Woman with Her Baby Monkey, N.J. 1971, Woman with a Fur Collar on the Street, N.Y.C. 1968, Woman in Her Negligee, N.Y.C. 1966, A Widow in Her Bedroom, N.Y.C. 1963,* all in *Diane Arbus* (Millerton, N.Y.: Aperture, 1972).

becomes more apparent. Arbus succeeded in pulling out or imposing upon her subjects a near-uniform anxiety or sadness, thus confirming common assumptions about the behavior and appearance of older women. There is little joy or serenity in her subjects' presentation of self to the camera. (This could also be said of most of Arbus's other subjects as well: her war supporters, for example, are almost parodies of wide-eyed fanatics; her teen-agers as mindless-looking as the most misanthropic youth-hater could hope; her cross-dressers as pathetic and self-deluded-looking as a Jerry Falwell could pray.) Compelling as these portraits are, I find something essentially mean-spirited in their premise—the seeking-out of subjects whose poverty, witlessness, class, in-experience, or traditional female deference made them easy targets for a strong-willed artist to impose herself upon. In none of Arbus's published work does one sense (with the possible exception of *Woman on a Park Bench on a Sunny Day,* who looks at the camera with a quizzing self-knowledge strikingly different from that of Arbus's other subjects) that she photographed people whom she considered her peers. And while it is pointless to wish that she had, the fact that she did not is a large factor in the sense of distance and the imposition of a uniform vision onto those people she did choose to portray: her vision of them was simply stronger than their own ability to project an alternative presentation of self. In this sense, Arbus's portraits are expres-sionistic, using the human countenance primarily as a plastic medium for conveying the artist's own feelings.

Richard Avedon, the 1970s' other gallery- and museum-certified por-traitist, strikes me as similarly narrow in his work. While disparaging the notion of celebrity as anything glamorous, his portraits nonetheless depend on this very quality of fame as the ironic counterbalance to their palpable mortality. Avedon rigorously excludes such telling details of character as ex-pressive gesture, possessions, setting from his work, leaving us with a pore-level anatomy of the subject that simultaneously declares his subjects' tran-scendence of identification-through-context (these subjects are *author, painter, Warhol superstar*)—their claim to immortality—and their pure physicality (and hence mortality). As in Arbus's portraits, Avedon's own assertion (*i.e.,* that even in the midst of life we are at death) imposes itself rigidly upon his subjects.

Because Noggle is committed to a broader imperative than the objec-tification of her own feelings, her work shows a greater variety of approach

to her subjects. If she sometimes imposes her own will, her private fantasies
onto a willing subject, it is to suggest a new way of viewing aging people
that justifies itself visually and imaginatively:

> I hope that all of my images have or hold in some sense the
> heroics of confronting life—I hope I speak more of immortality,
> of humanness and that our limited spans on this planet are
> notable. I'm trying to humanize the middle-aged and older, to
> find a new perspective that does more than simply deny older
> persons and let them be a viable part of society. I cannot view life
> as a tragedy alone—certainly what sees you through is humor and
> recognition of the banality of the whole time-span and the
> nobility of it, too.

Anne Noggle lives alone. The portraits she has made fill the walls of her
working space, silent partners to her life.

> I know I shouldn't say this, but I like my own photographs. I
> like to go into the room where they hang and turn the music up
> and have a drink and play a game of pool with myself at 11 P.M.
> and look up and see them. I feel good with them—they're like
> friends and I'm happy in their company.

Janice Zita Grover

Columbia College, Chicago
1983

Seeing Ourselves

From a Speech Delivered to the Class of 1983,
Portland School of Art, Maine

I have been thinking about you . . . and about what I could tell you that might come back to you at some time when you especially needed a lift. In truth I didn't know whether to talk about art or peanut butter sandwiches! They both feed us. The real feast is life itself, and since I've lived the greater part of mine I though I'd ruminate about how I've gotten from there to here.

I was born in a suburb of Chicago during the Great Depression, and grew up wanting two things—to fly airplanes and to go west. I did both. I soloed while still in high school, and when I turned twenty-one I became a Woman's Air Force Service Pilot in World War II. I towed targets for gunnery, and I would turn down the big mirror meant to alert pilots of enemy planes, to see myself flying that fighter plane. It made it seem real in a different way, seeing myself being there. I flew airplanes for a living for eleven years and 6,000 hours.

I was at home in a plane—a machine if you like—I learned procedures, blindfolded cockpit checks, instrument flying, acrobatics, how to talk with my hands . . . and I gained command of the plane. I could make it perform, do its stuff. Reactions became quick and automatic. Then it was freedom, and at that point you just strapped yourself to the machine and it became a part of you. You would think "I want to go over there," or look at the world in a spin, have it float by inverted or whatever. The mastery was always a means to something else. When I was twenty-five I became a stunt pilot with an air show; when I was twenty-six I became a crop-duster pilot. When I was thirty-one I decided I wanted to see the world so I went on active duty in the Air Force as an intercept controller. When I was thirty-six I was in Paris as a protocol officer. I discovered art there. When I was thirty-seven I was disability-retired from the service.

When I was thirty-eight I was a freshman in college, majoring in art history. When I was forty-three I took a course in photography. I fell passionately in love with another machine, the camera. Like the flying machine you have to be attentive to the mechanics of it; then you are again free in your mind to act and think about images. You see through the viewfinder but also through your experience and through whatever synthesis your mind has formed from those experiences. Living, in itself, doesn't have a value for you as an artist unless what you have thought and done—the fright and delight and the gin and sin and children and morning light and all the rest— ride in your insides and ferment and come together. Then one day you are, as I am now, up here, speaking with the voice that has called the control tower in Eagle Pass, Texas, using these hands that have so recently held that camera in Seattle, Washington, standing on these feet that loved to dance in the Aragon Ballroom in Chicago—and it all makes sense and it all adds up. I am alive and well and living in Albuquerque.

It didn't just add up that way by slogging through life looking at my feet. I would like to quote the screenwriter Garson Kanin, who said *"Amateurs hope, professionals work."* I would also like to quote myself when I wrote what has turned out to be a kind of credo for me: *"I am filled with dread that I will wake up and find I have become a completely rational being, with a finite set of values, within whose framework I must find my manners and dream my dreams."*

I could have offered you many pronouncements that were all true but lacked the spirit of what really goes on inside us, the real truth, the difference between what we say we are and what we are really about in our innermost selves. So now I just want to tell you how we have to create our own world— a kind of secret place. I thought I would create myself in a Walter Mitty- like way . . . the self as hero and protagonist. We don't have time to do everything, but we can experience it through our imagination.

I could tell you about living in Paris . . . how finally I realized I could barely breathe and couldn't even care about eating and watched myself become thin and shake so badly I couldn't even get the toothpaste on the brush. The Air Force couldn't figure out what was the matter with me. I looked on myself with wonder and decided that I probably was going to die.

I could tell you how I flew home from Europe on an Air Force plane, and all night I would open my eyes and look at the new captain's bars gleaming on my shoulders and saying in my head "Je suis Capitaine Noggle"; the idea of that and the ocean and the sky and the sense of aloneness remains as a romantic image in my head to this day.

And how I was in this plane in World War II and intentionally spun it. It was way out of rig and wouldn't stop spinning, and I tried to get out and found the centrifugal force too strong to even move so I decided that if I were going to die, I would die trying and then did everything they had told us not to do with the controls and the plane came out of the spin just sort of tumbling around in the sky. And how I shook after I landed, and no one else even noticed the miracle of my being still here on earth.

When I was too young to read I used to plague my sister to read me the story of "The Little Engine That Could." It was a rusty small engine that only had one chance for success and love. It chugged up the mountain saying, "I hope I can, I hope I can, I think I can, I think I can, I know I can, I know I can." Every time she read me the story my heart would beat harder and harder. I won't admit that way down inside I probably associate myself with that little rusty thing.

And how I love the Ginsberg poem, "Sunflower Sutra," about the spiky soot-covered sunflower on a trash heap alongside the railroad track. In the poem Ginsberg finally holds it up and says "A perfect beauty of a sunflower! A perfect excellent lovely sunflower existence! . . ./How many flies buzzed round you innocent of your grime while you cursed the heavens of the railroad and your flower soul?/Poor dead flower? when did you forget you were a flower? when did you look at your skin and decide you were an impotent dirty old locomotive? . . . the specter and shade of a once powerful mad American locomotive?/You were never no locomotive, Sunflower, you were a sun-flower! . . . —We're not our skin of grime, we're not our dread bleak dusty imageless locomotive, we're all beautiful golden sunflowers inside."

I could tell you about my first lung surgery, when courage wasn't a matter of instant response, of coolness in the face of danger, but that long haul of knowing and waiting. I had always wondered how I would do when it wasn't just a glamorous big event. I worried that I wouldn't do it well, and how relieved I was to find that I could do that too (except when I awakened in the night soaking wet, but you can't control your unconscious).

In World War II I found out someone I loved had gone down in his plane in the North Sea with no survivors. And I made a pledge to go there someday, and thirty-six years later I hired a boat at Whitby, England. The weather was stormy, but I didn't have another day to try again, so we went out into the North Sea and I thought about him and then let that go. My 1982 verbal image of what my photographic imagery is about is called "Sketch for a Self Portrait" and it goes like this:

> Where are you tonight while the sky reflects my solitary
>   presence.
> Where are you now, those of you who might whisper I love you,
> are you in a watery grave down under the sea with a picture of
>   me smiling in your hip pocket.
> Where did all the promise go where did all the friends go. Have
>   we dissolved into the past,
> are we granny or auntie or that old lady down the street. I have
>   lost my way
> and my face reminds me of that. Every stop and start, love and
>   loss legible.
> A whole individual story and who will read it.
> Who will look at my face and find me there?

Those are some of the ways my life has been my drama, and I its protagonist. It is from all those incidents of my life that I draw, and I am always aware that at the bottom of ourselves lies that awareness of our mortality. I am intrigued by the dichotomy of our individual mortality and our collective immortality. Our fragility, our toughness. That which bands us together and that which alienates us one from another. The look of us as we know more and lose our grip on that knowledge. The ritual of existence; the ascent and the descent. The voyage itself, trailing bloodlines, in the company of phantoms, inner visages, outer images, and the alterations of time.

I photograph people, most often older women, focusing on the tension between the iron determinant of age and the individual character of the subject. I try for images that get beneath the surface into that unchanging arena of the human psyche, formed in early life, which grows into maturity but does not relinquish its basic character throughout one's life. That deepest self, discernible only to one who is patient, watchful, and perhaps older oneself. The image I seek is of youth betrayed by age, of spirit strong but fragile with time. I want to show who the people in my pictures are, and how damned difficult it is as each of us in our time becomes them.

The nineteenth-century romantic ideal of the individual as the source of creativity took as a central metaphor the Aeolian harp—a wind harp that creates its own music. Postmodernism avows that the individual artist can no longer be seen as a creator but merely as a participant in the intellectual rumination of the times. If that is true, perhaps *seeing ourselves* is no more than a game. But the idea that everything that can be done by the individual has already been done is nonsense!

To look straight into a face and find the pulse of what it is to be human, that is what fuels me, that is the sum of my mind and my longing. I am always aware of our unceasing engagement with time and space—our ultimate limitations—translated into life and death. How wonderful it is to have meaning in our work—to have a life work that sustains us as we sustain it by our willing labor, and every now and then a reward like getting to be here in your time and space and having a chance to communicate with you.

Anne Noggle

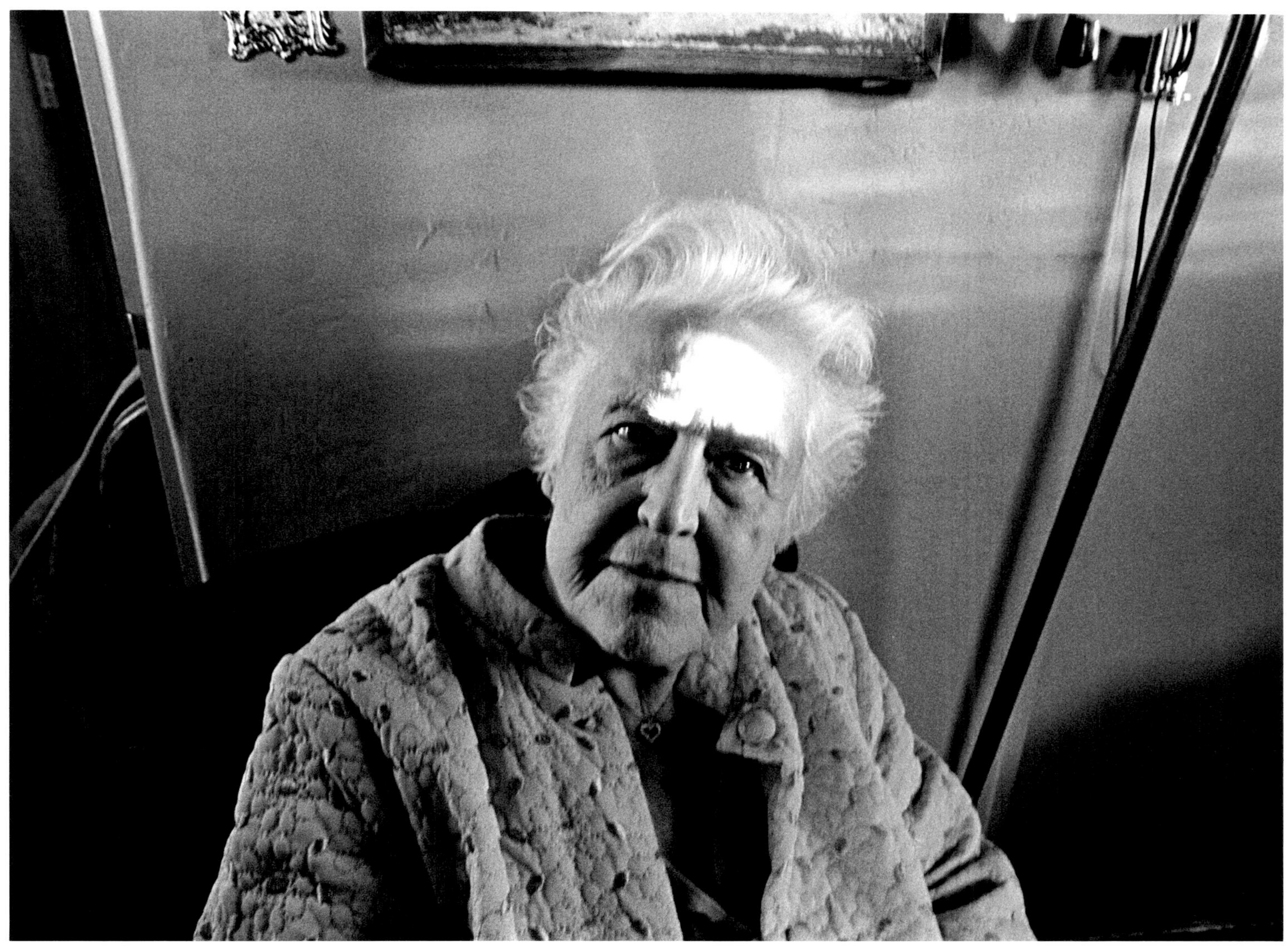

Agnes   1969

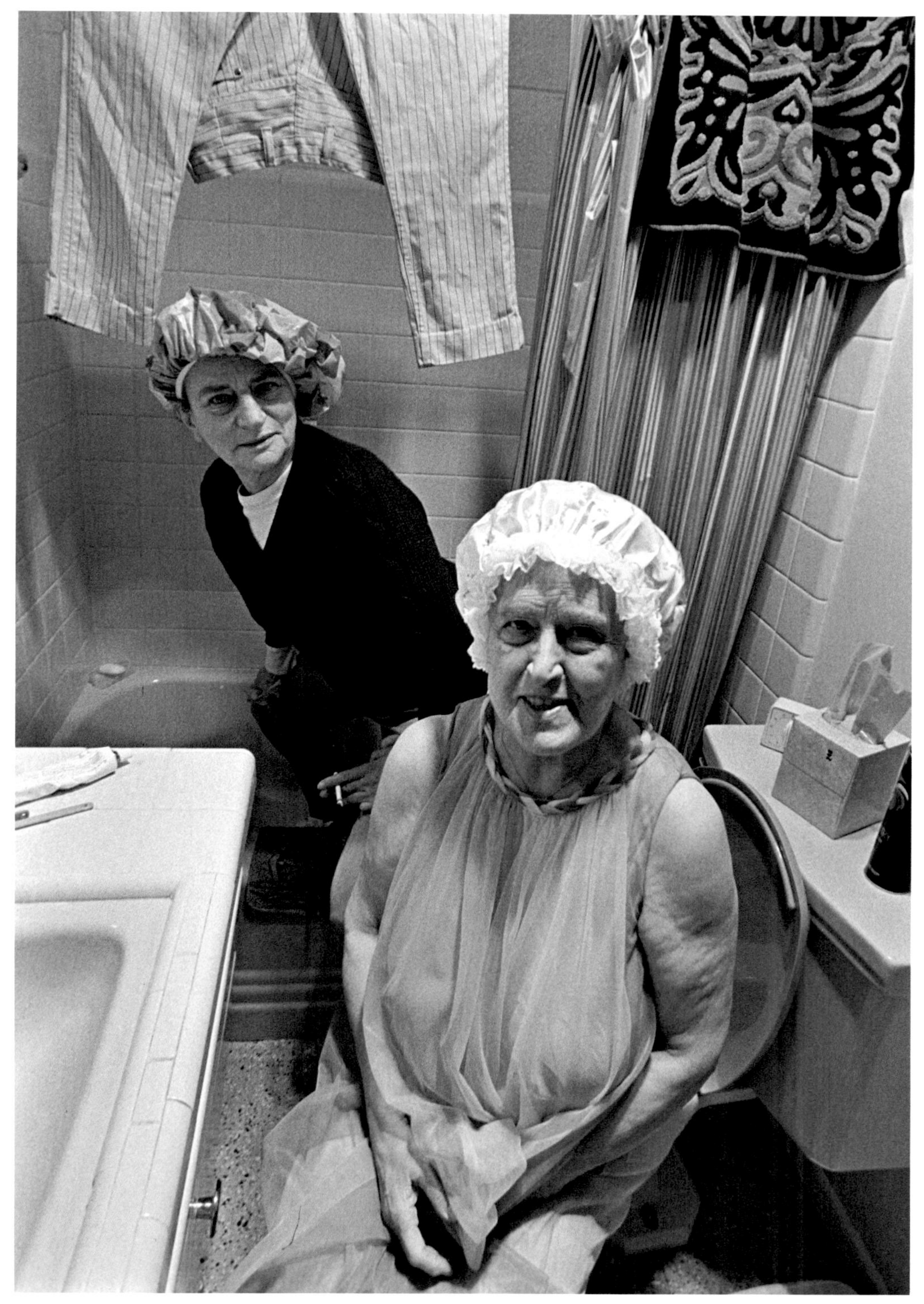

Agnes and Shelley   1970

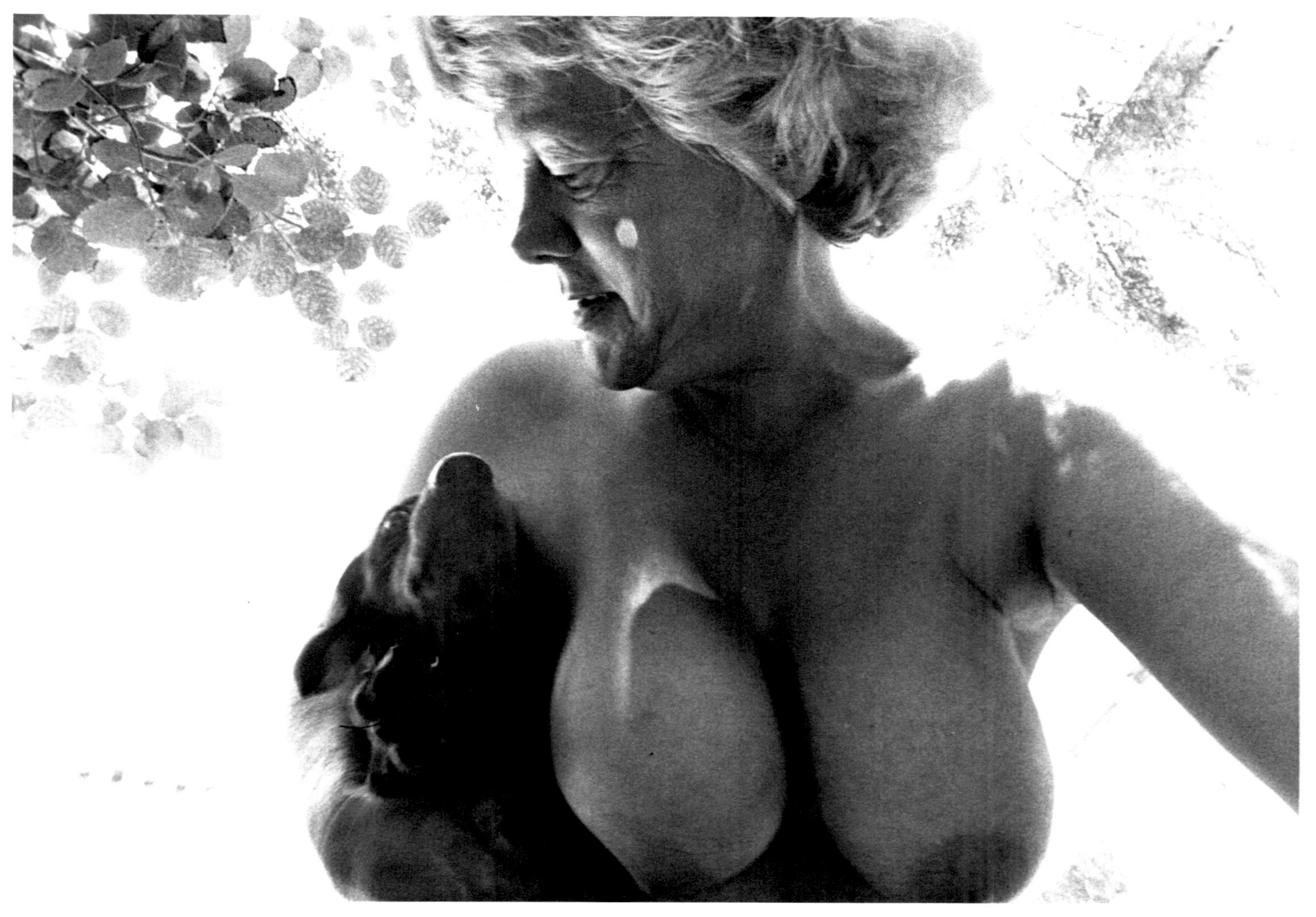

Self-portrait with Pepe   1970

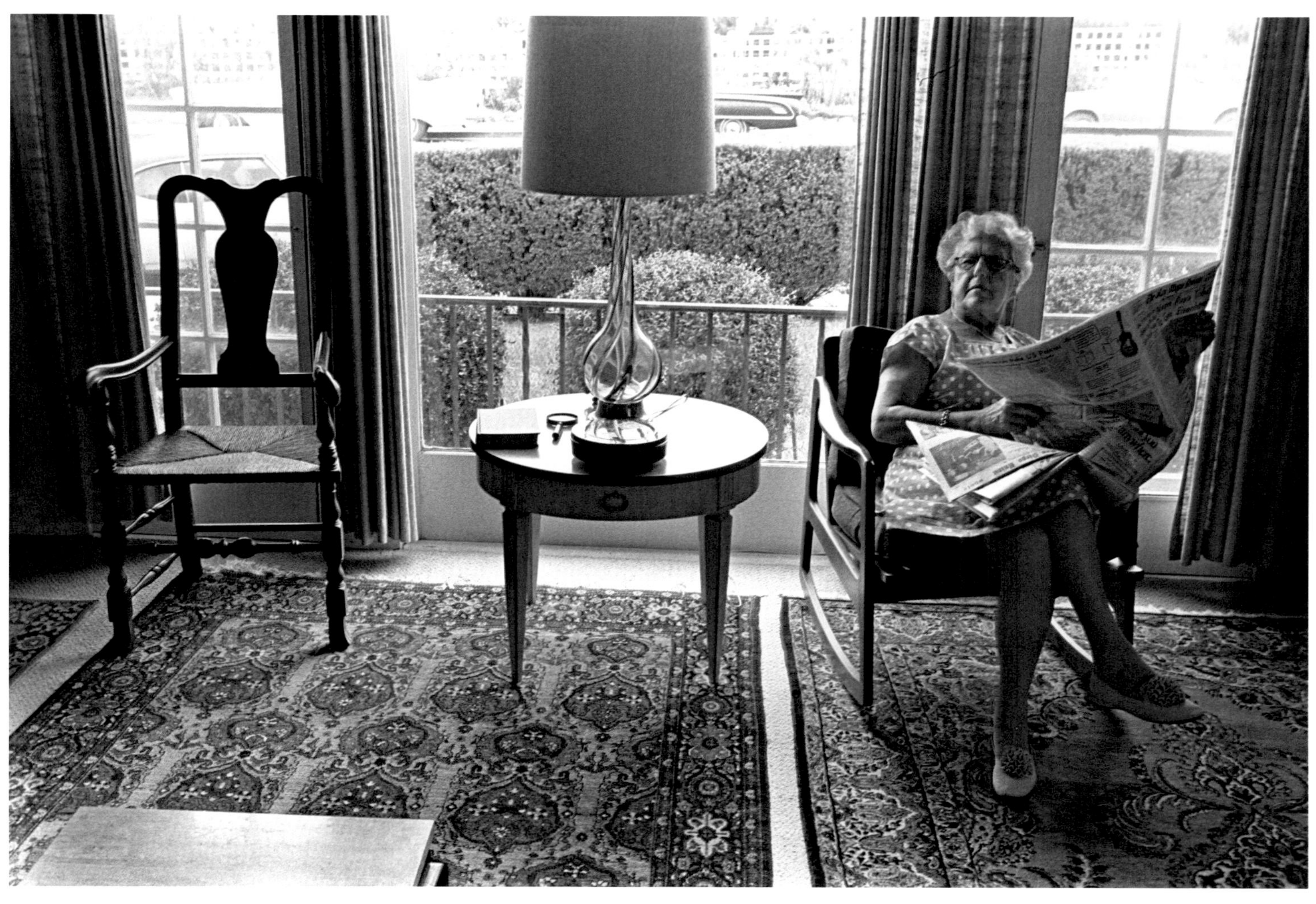

Agnes, La Jolla   1970

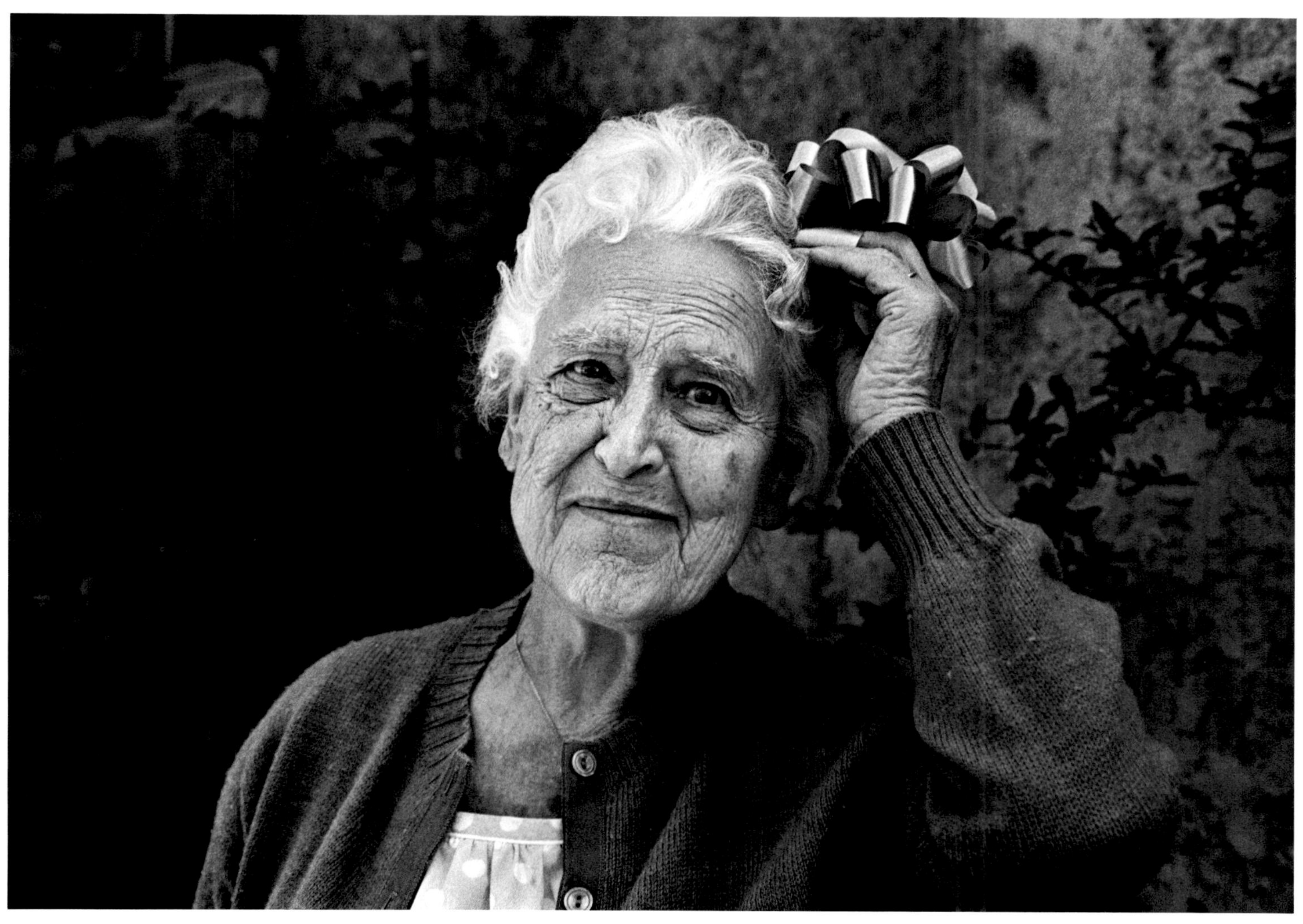

Agnes, 84th Birthday   1974

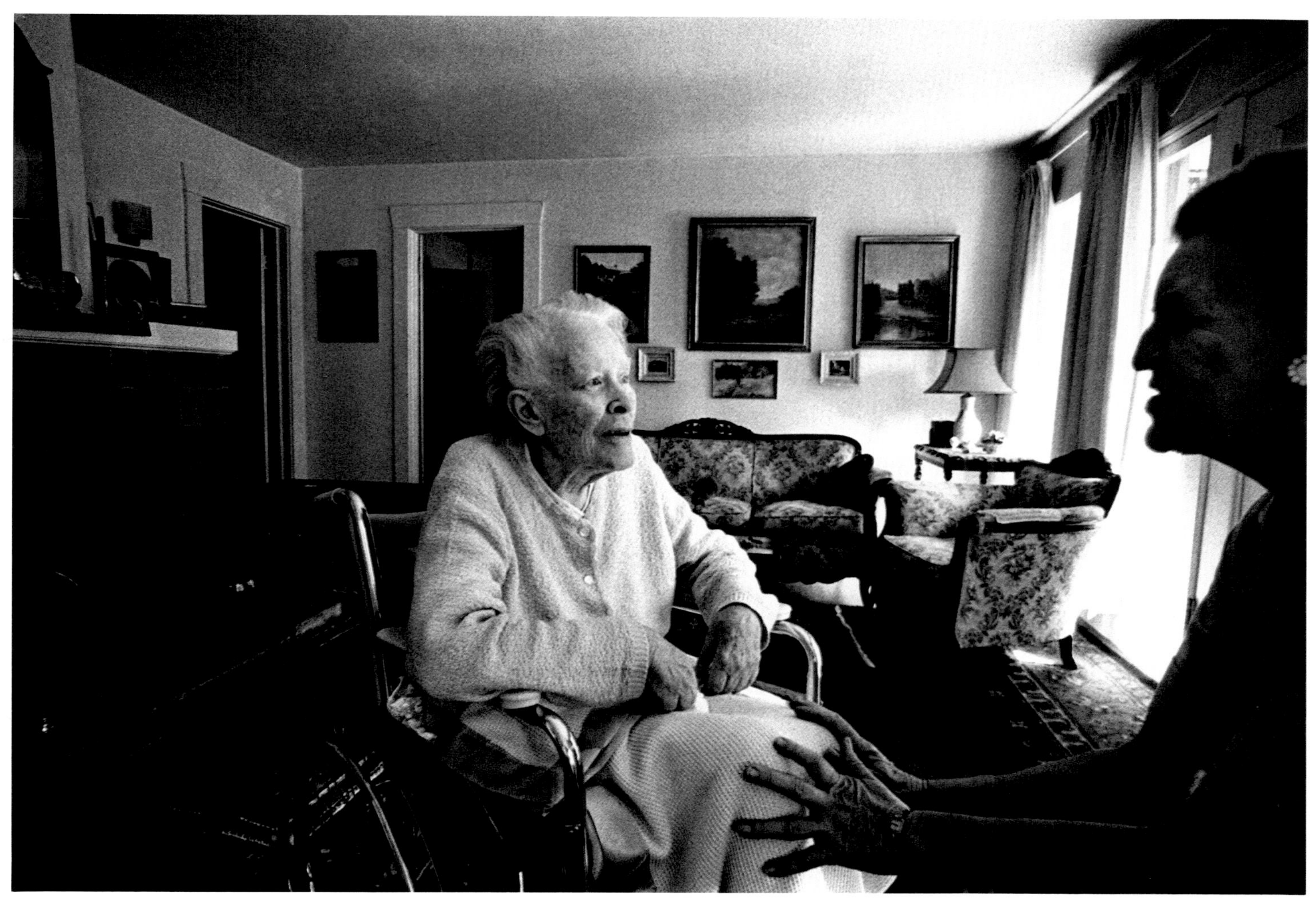

La Jolla No. 3   1975

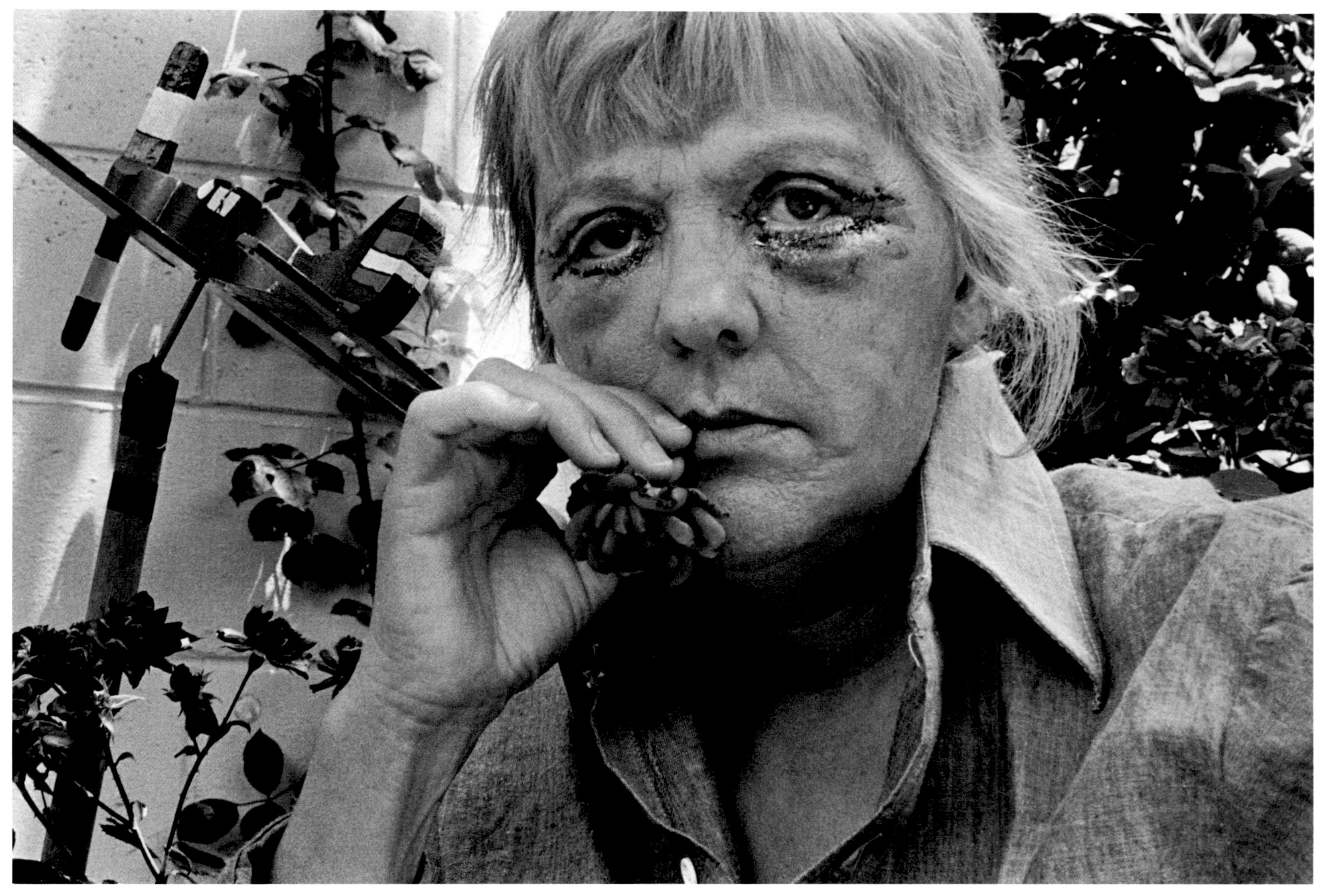

Face-lift No. 3   1975

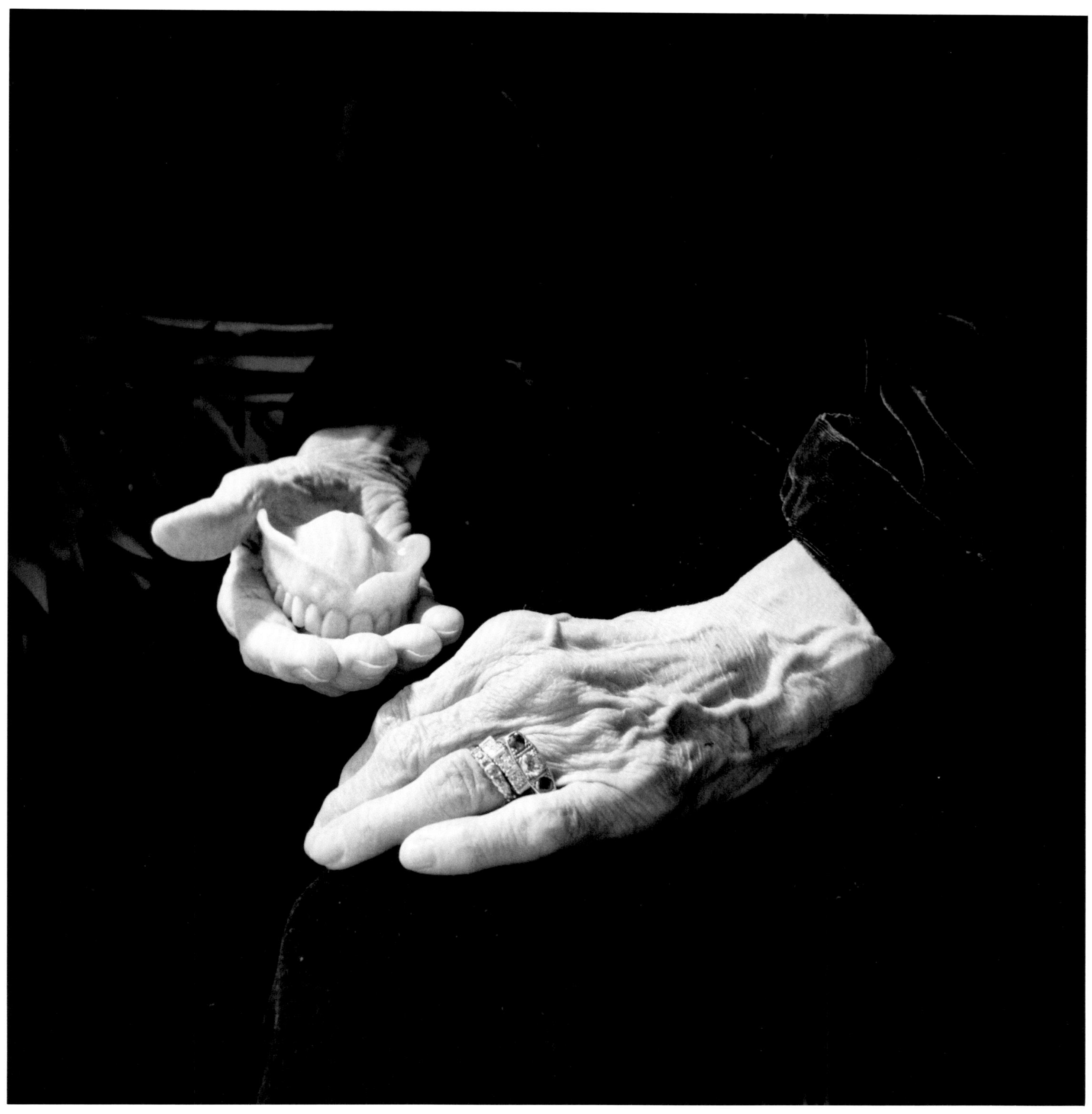

Artifact   1976

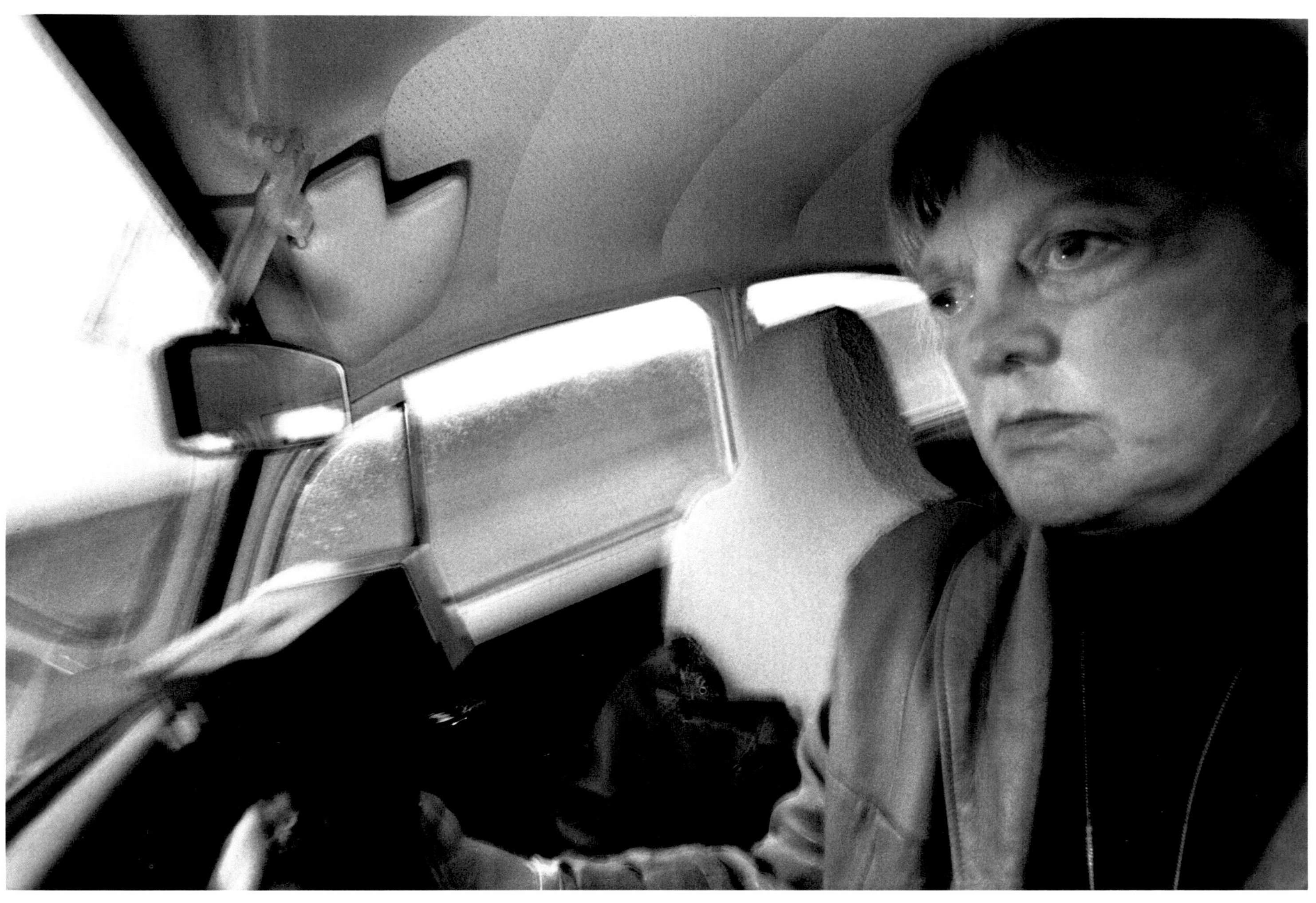

Self-portrait   1976

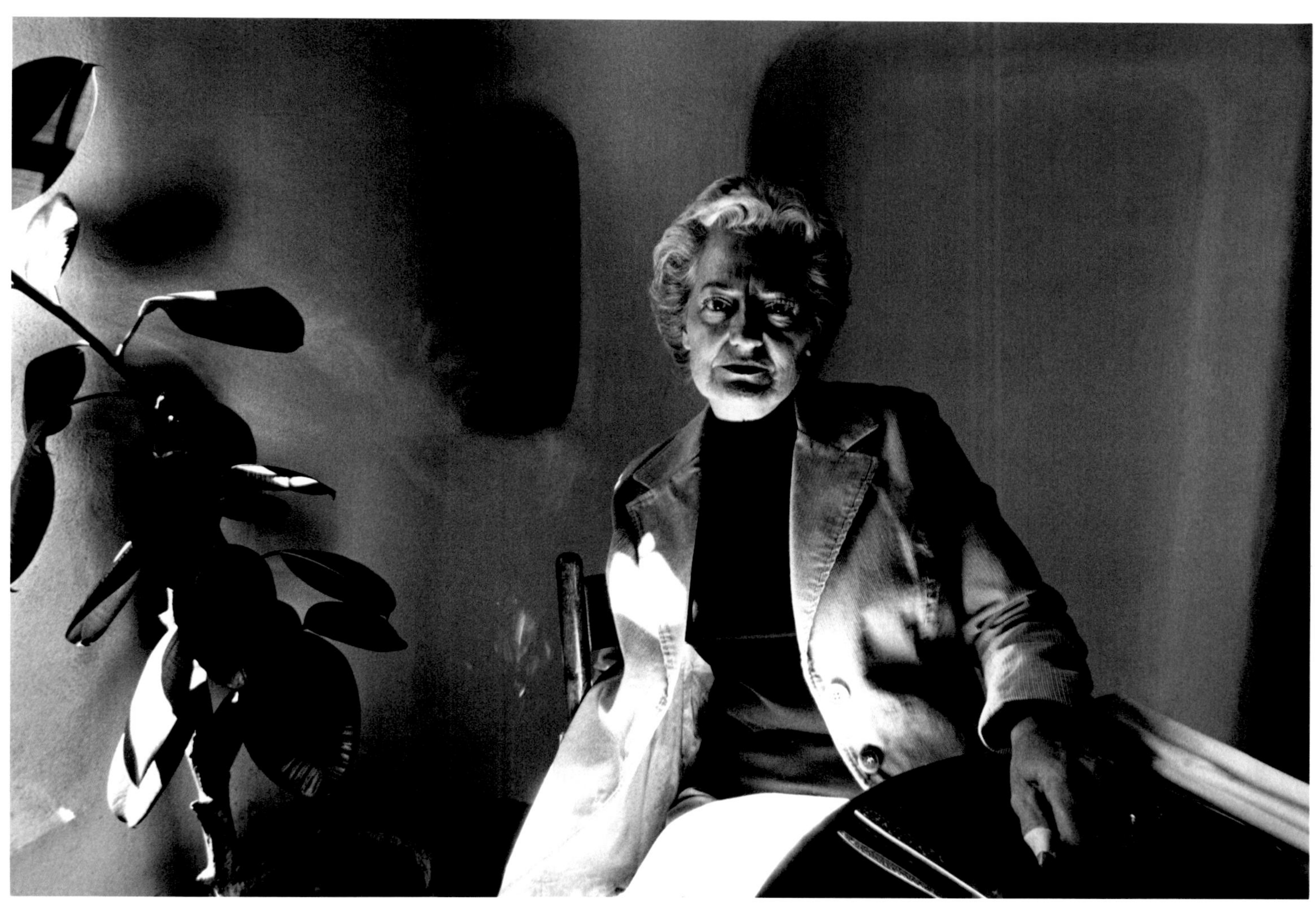

Mary, Afternoon November 1976

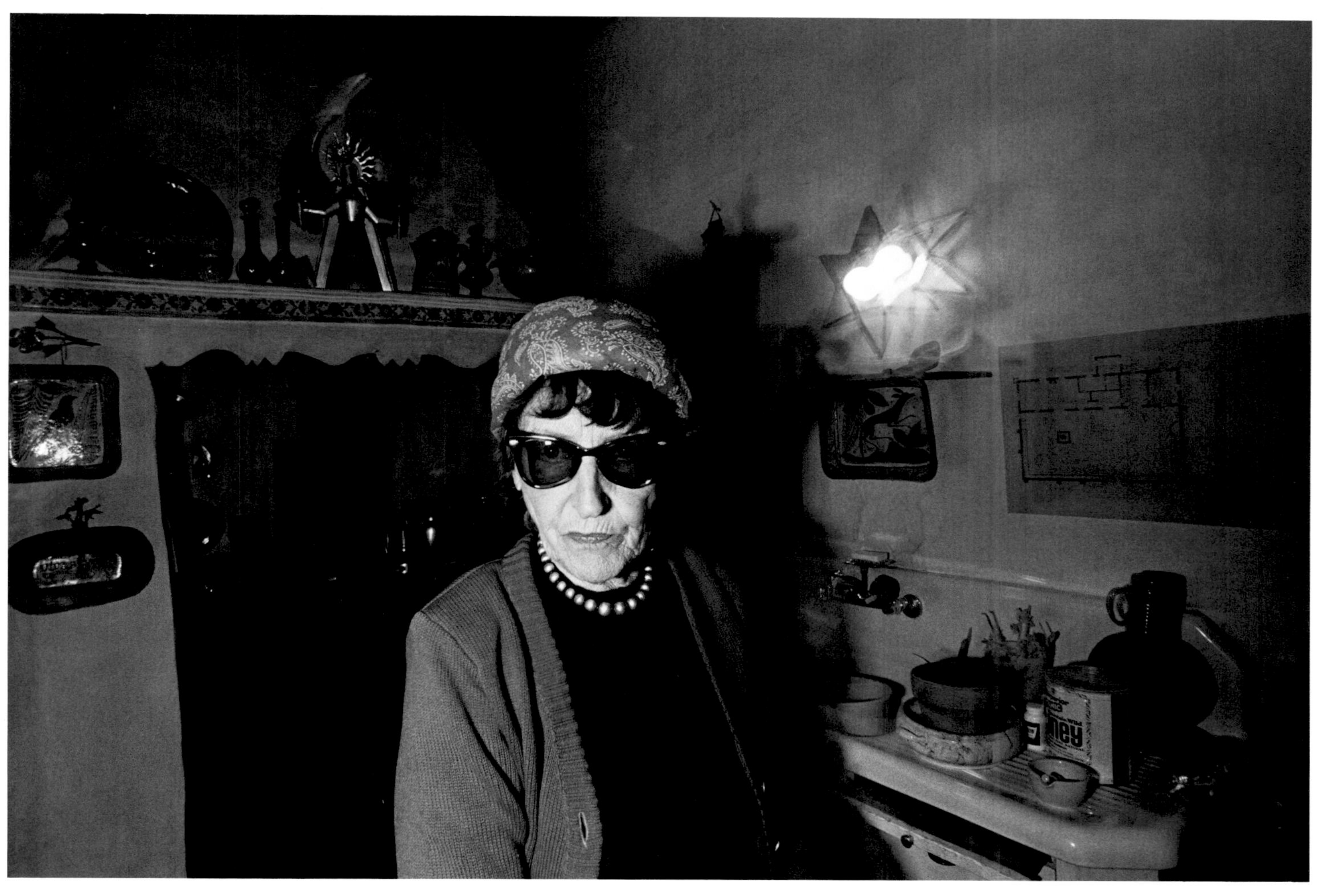

Santa Fe Spring 1976

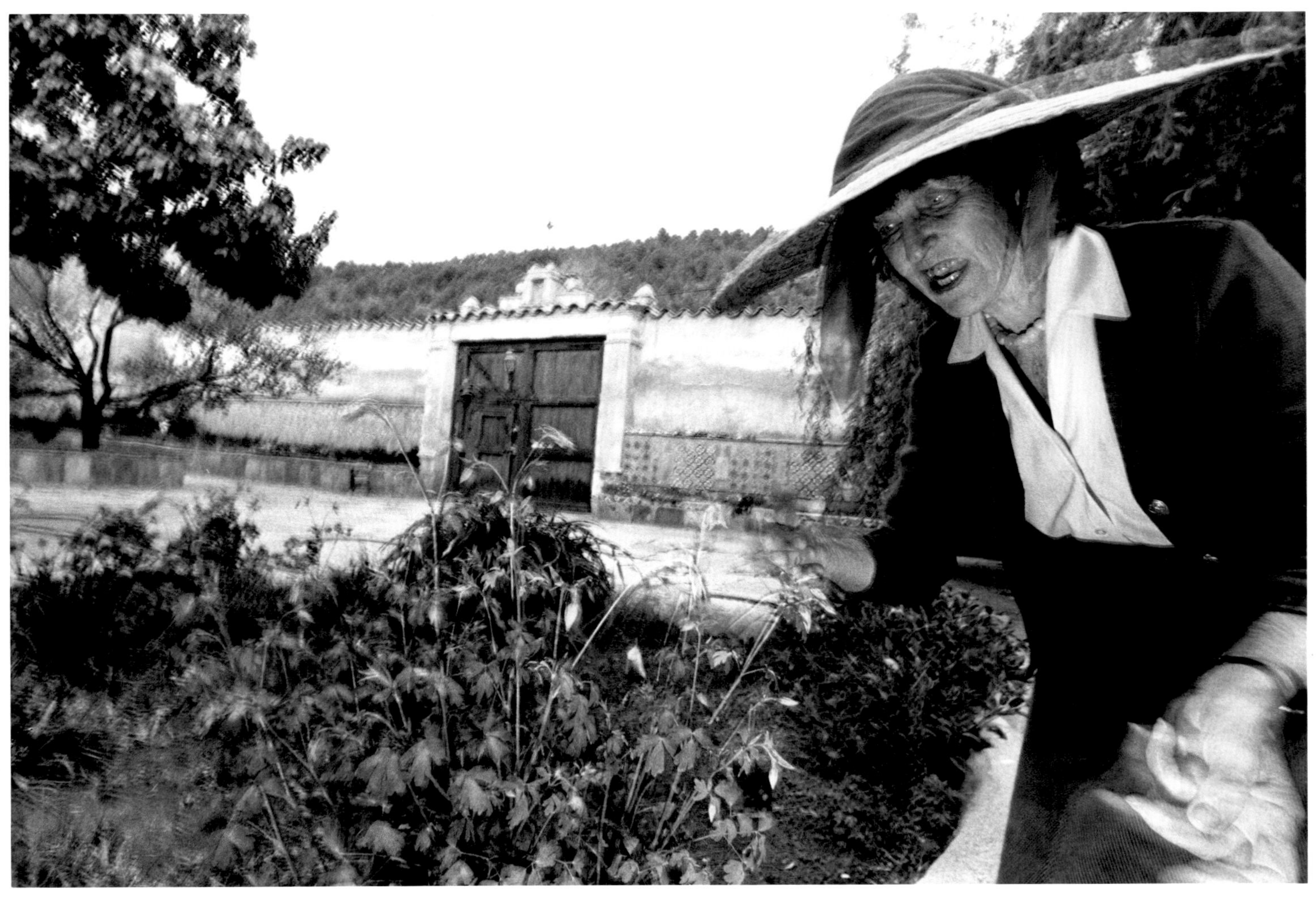

Santa Fe Summer No. 1   1976

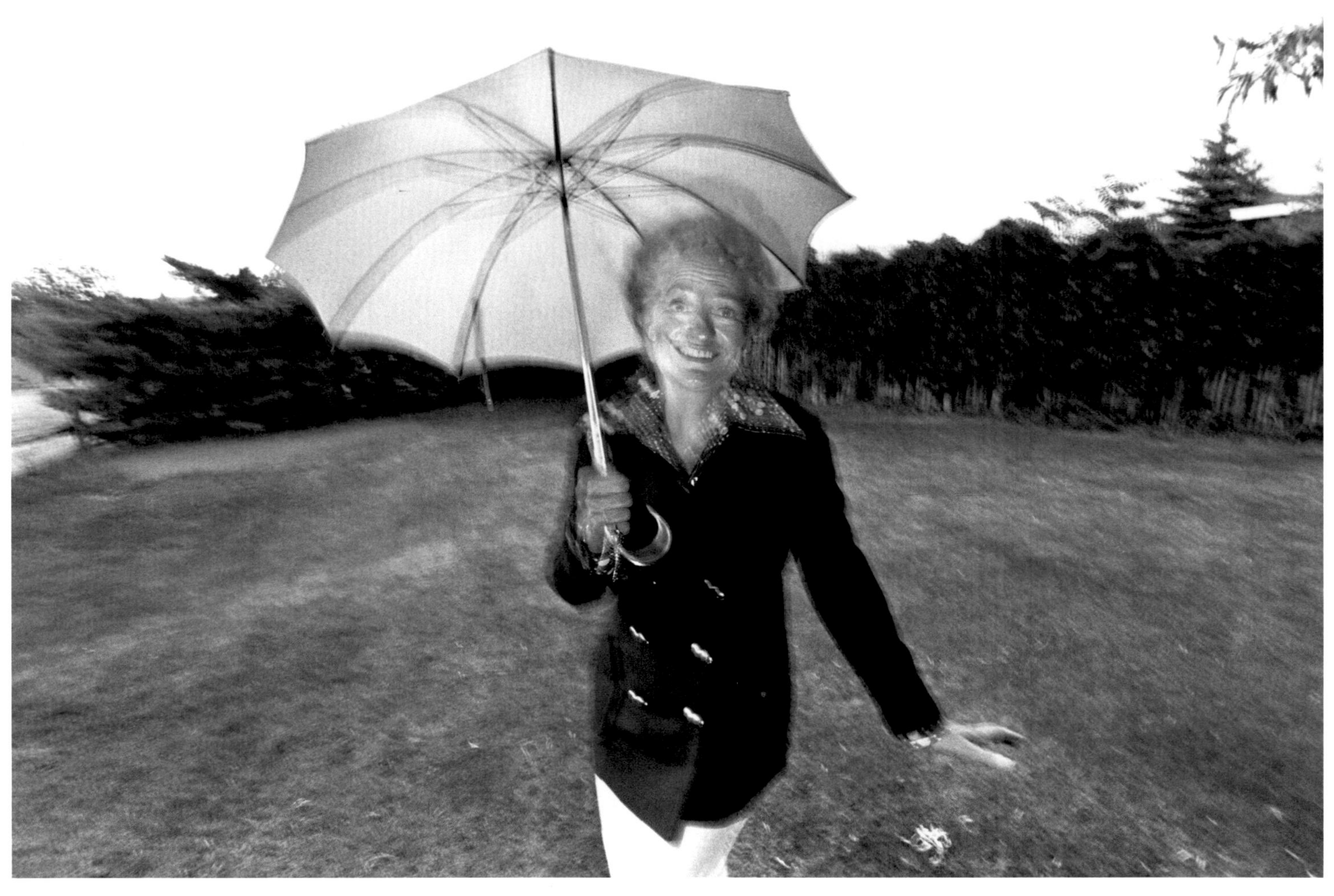

Santa Fe Summer No. 2   1976

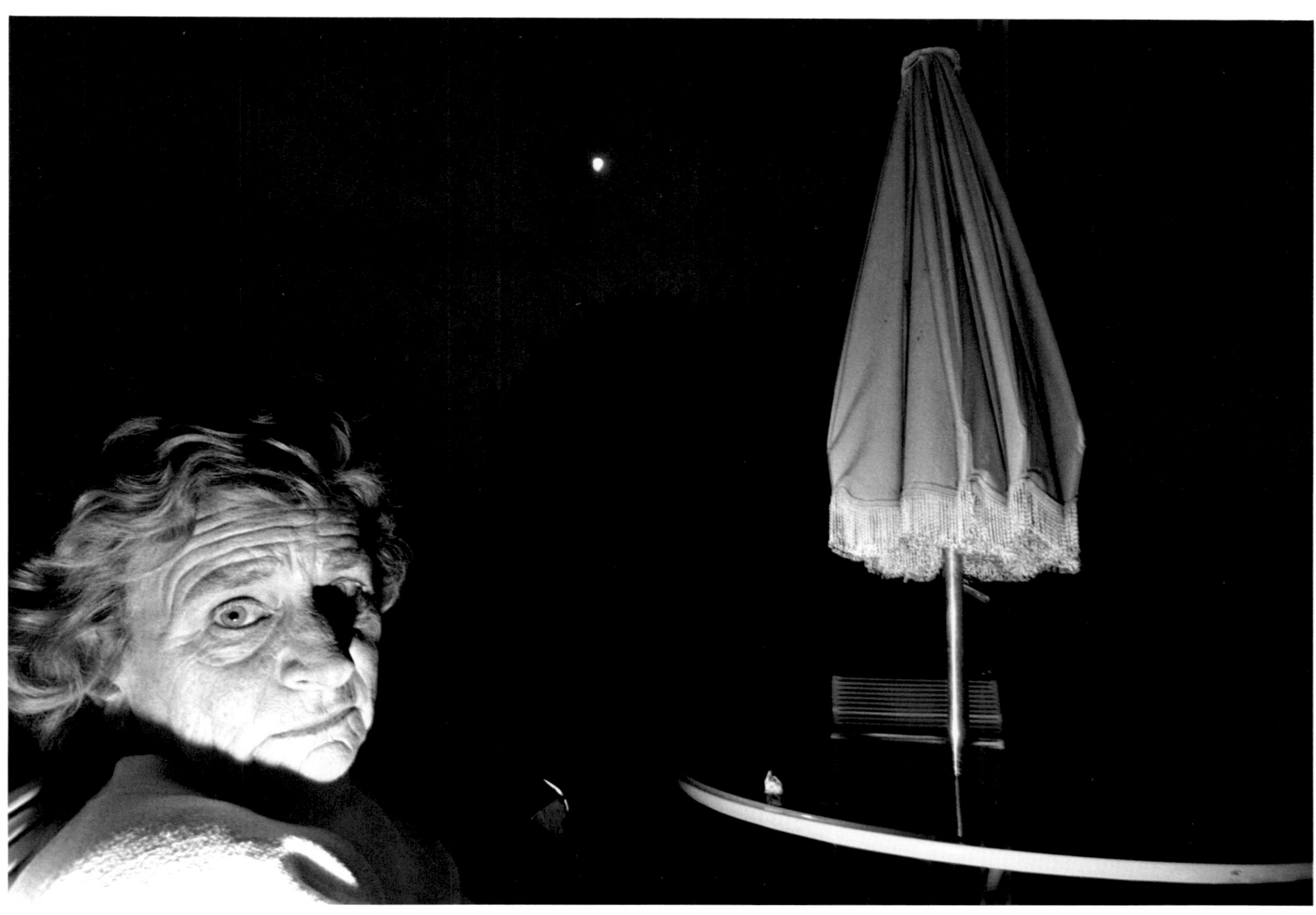

Moonlight over Albuquerque   1976

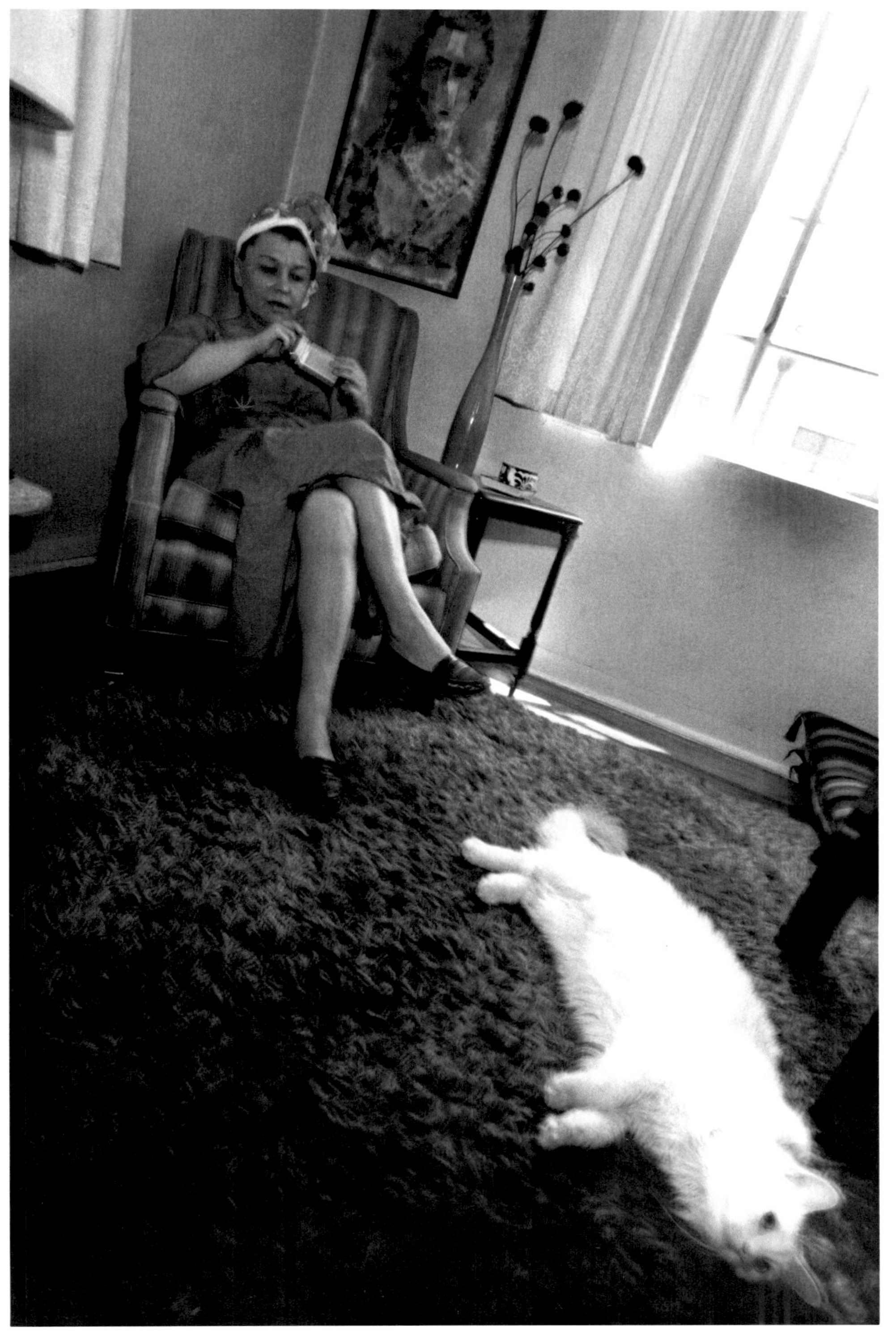

Morris   1976

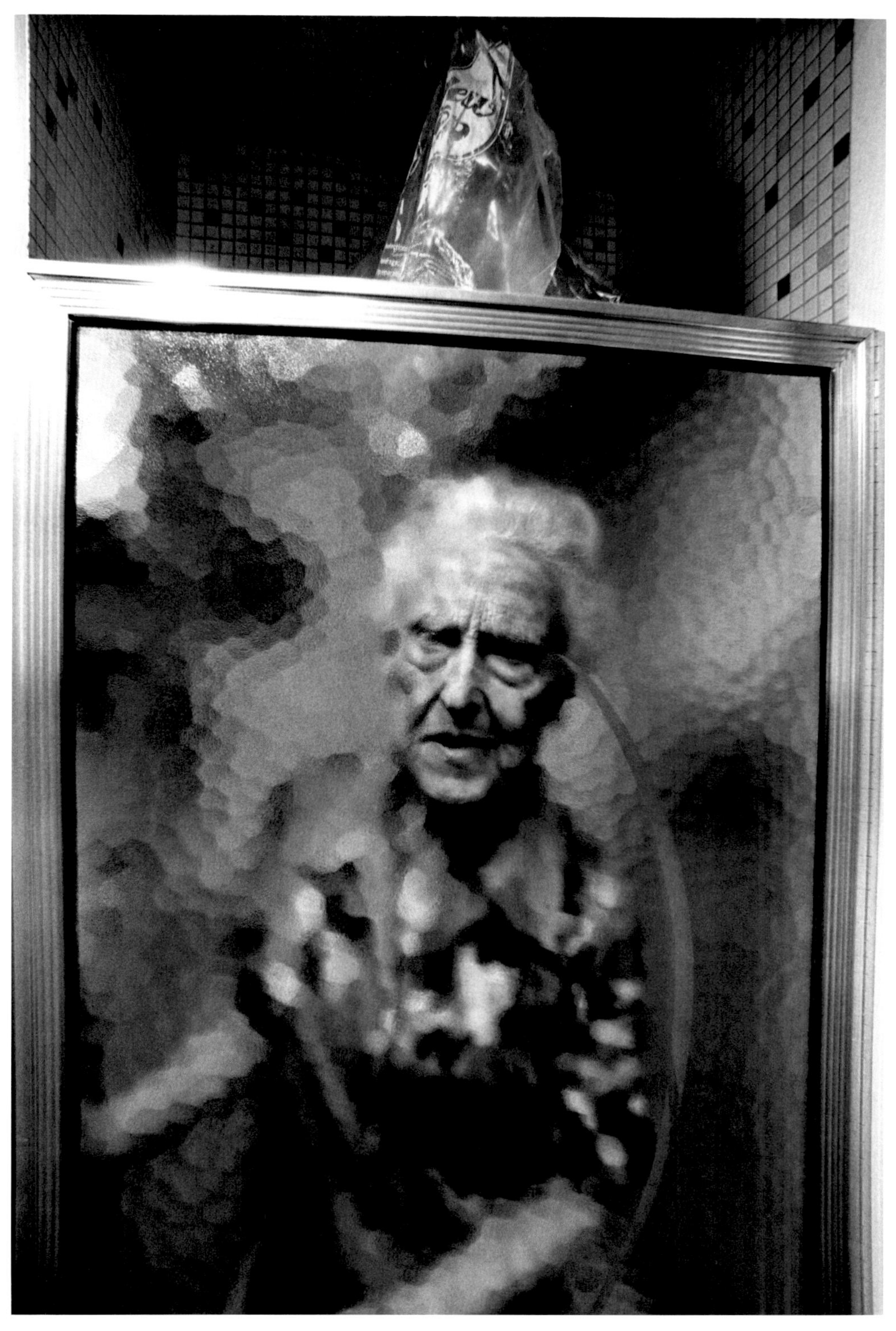

Agnes   1976

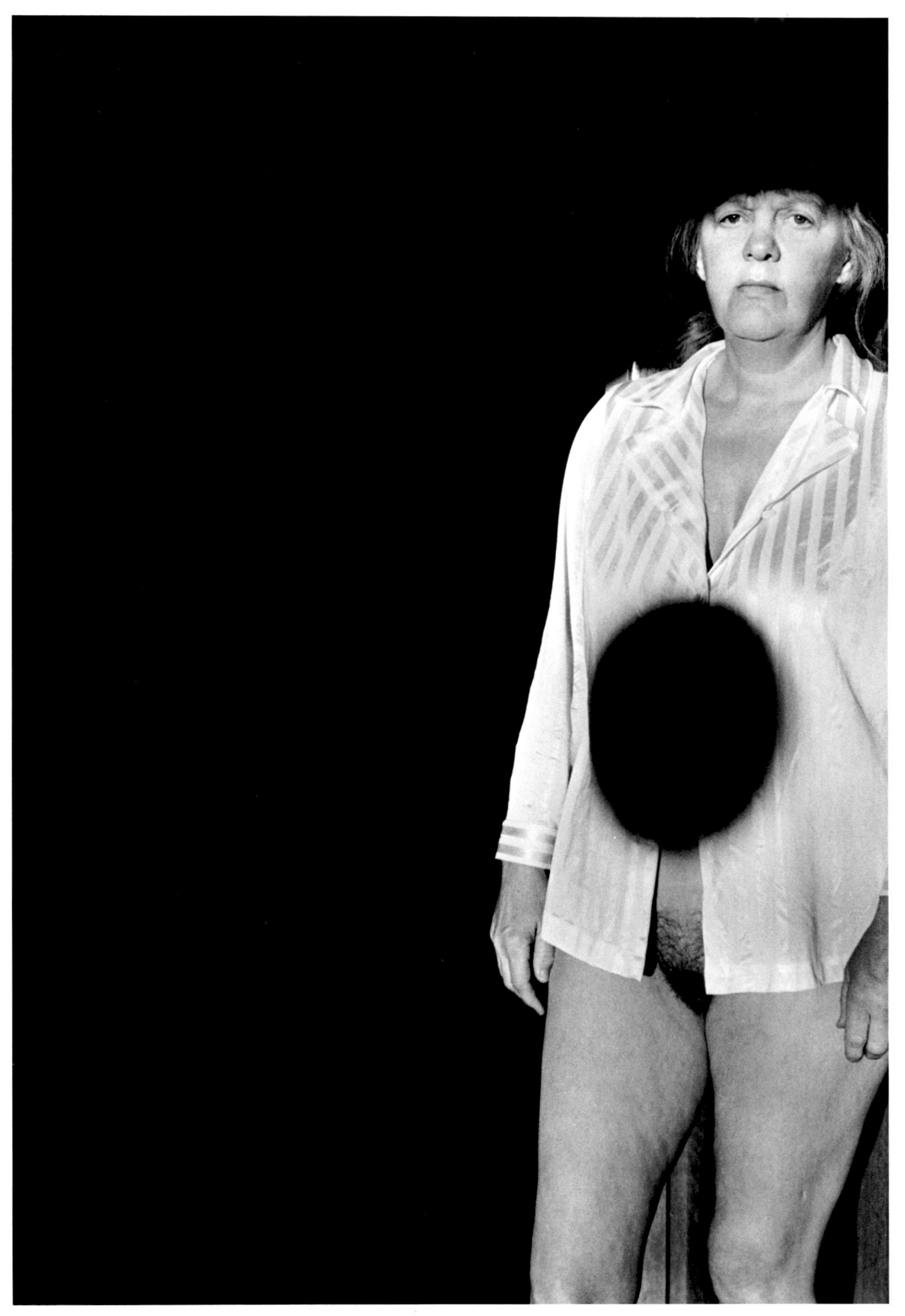

Myself, 7 A.M.   1977

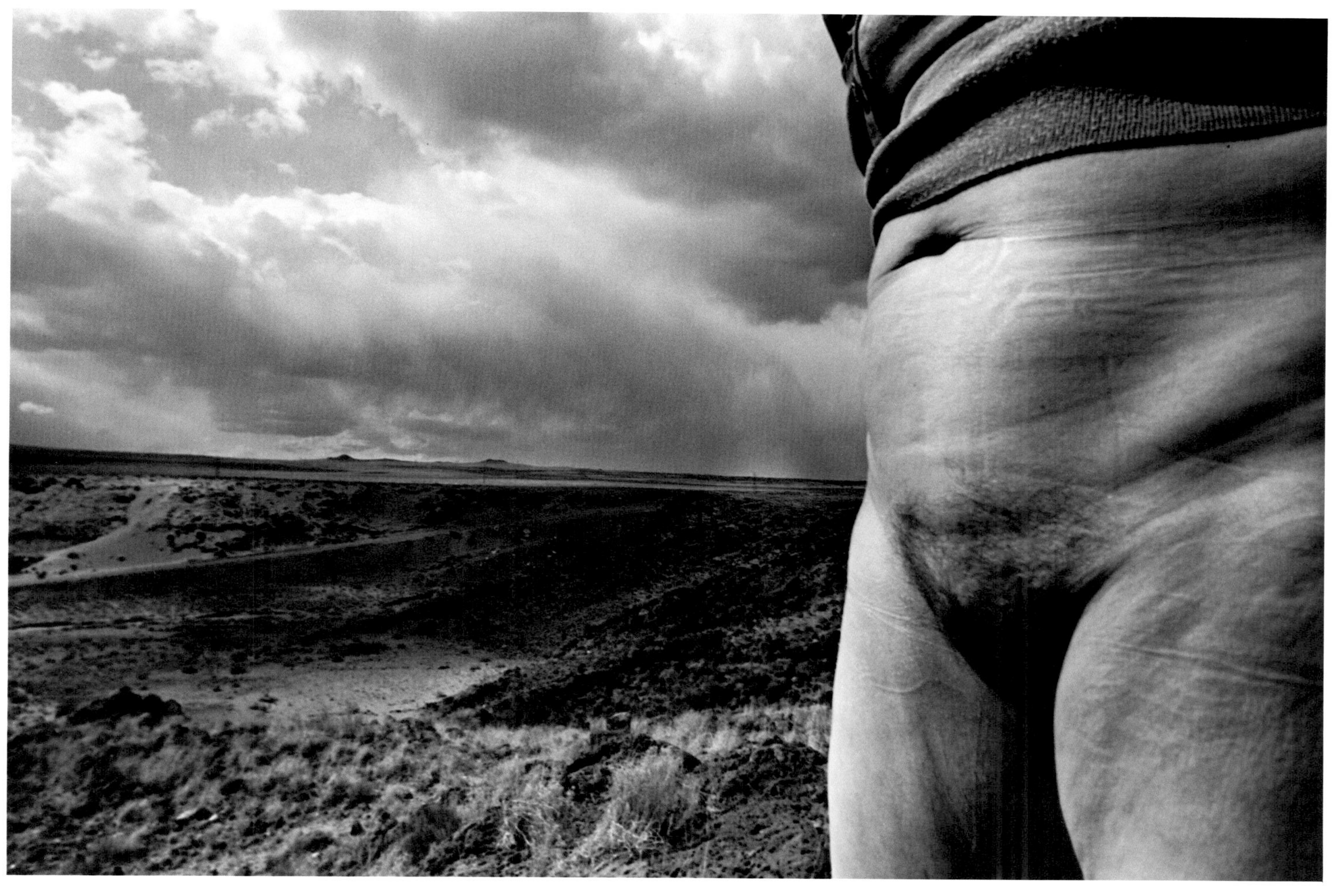

Stonehenge Decoded   1977

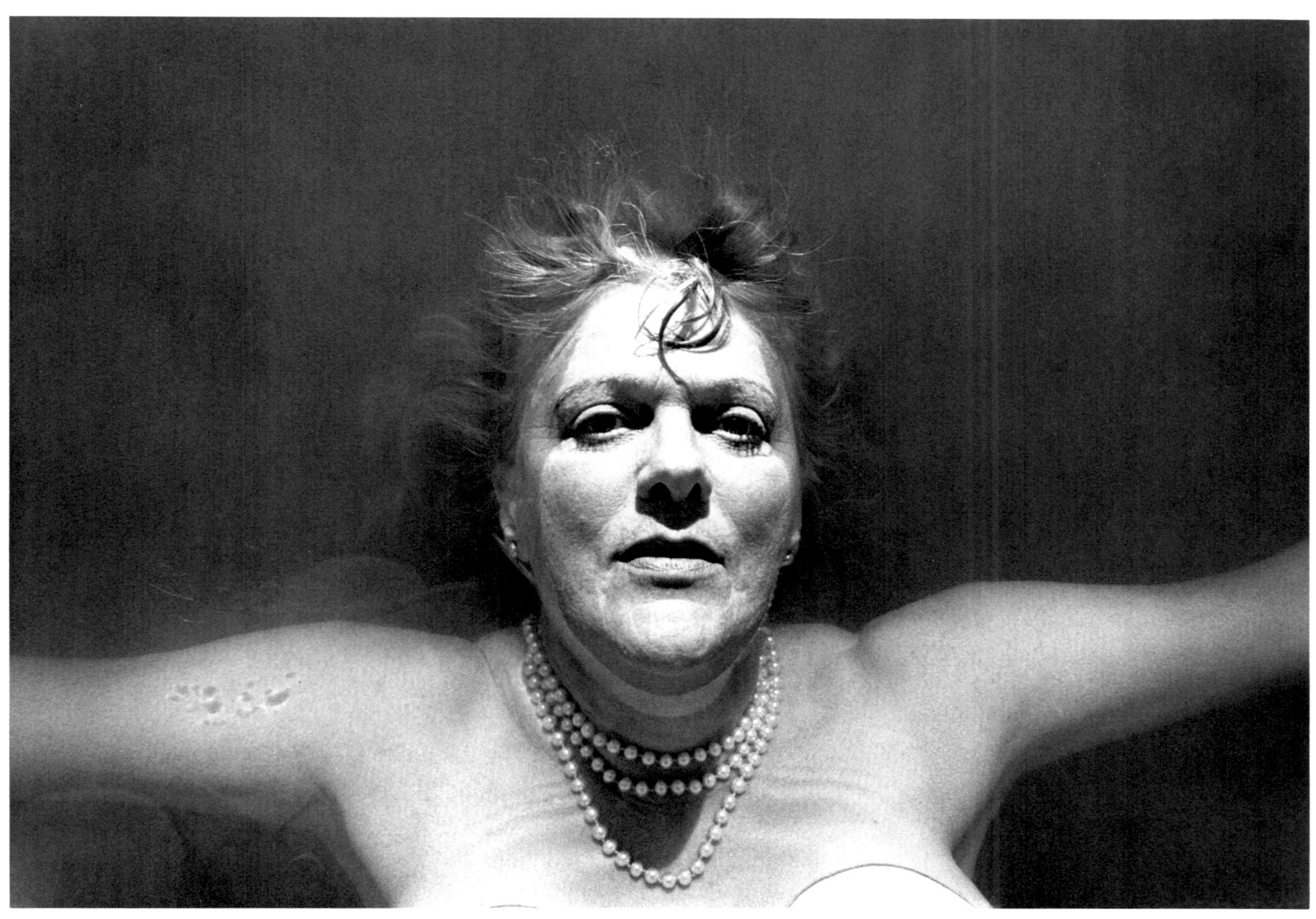

Self-image in Cochiti Lake   1978

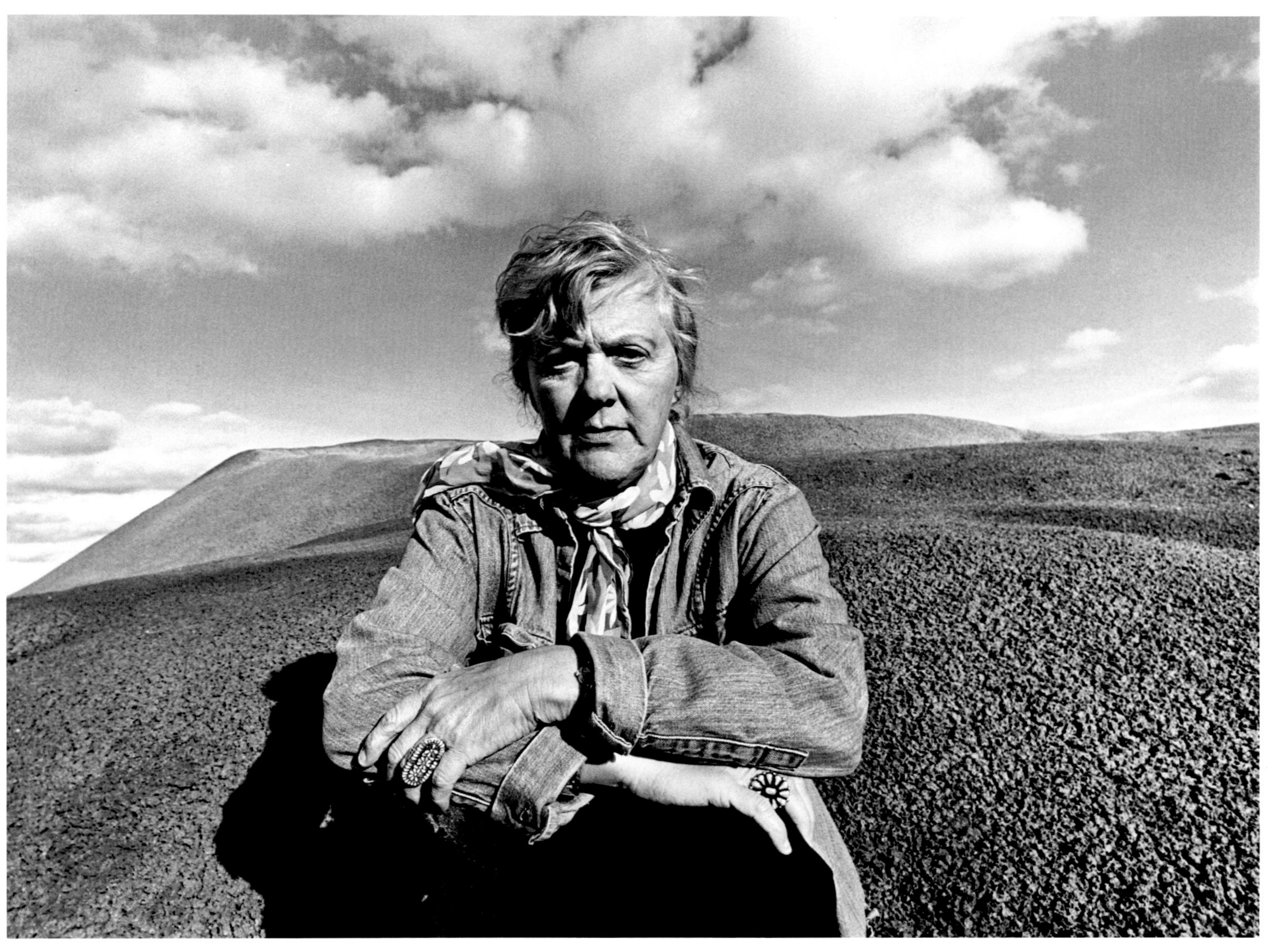

Self-Image No. 2   1978

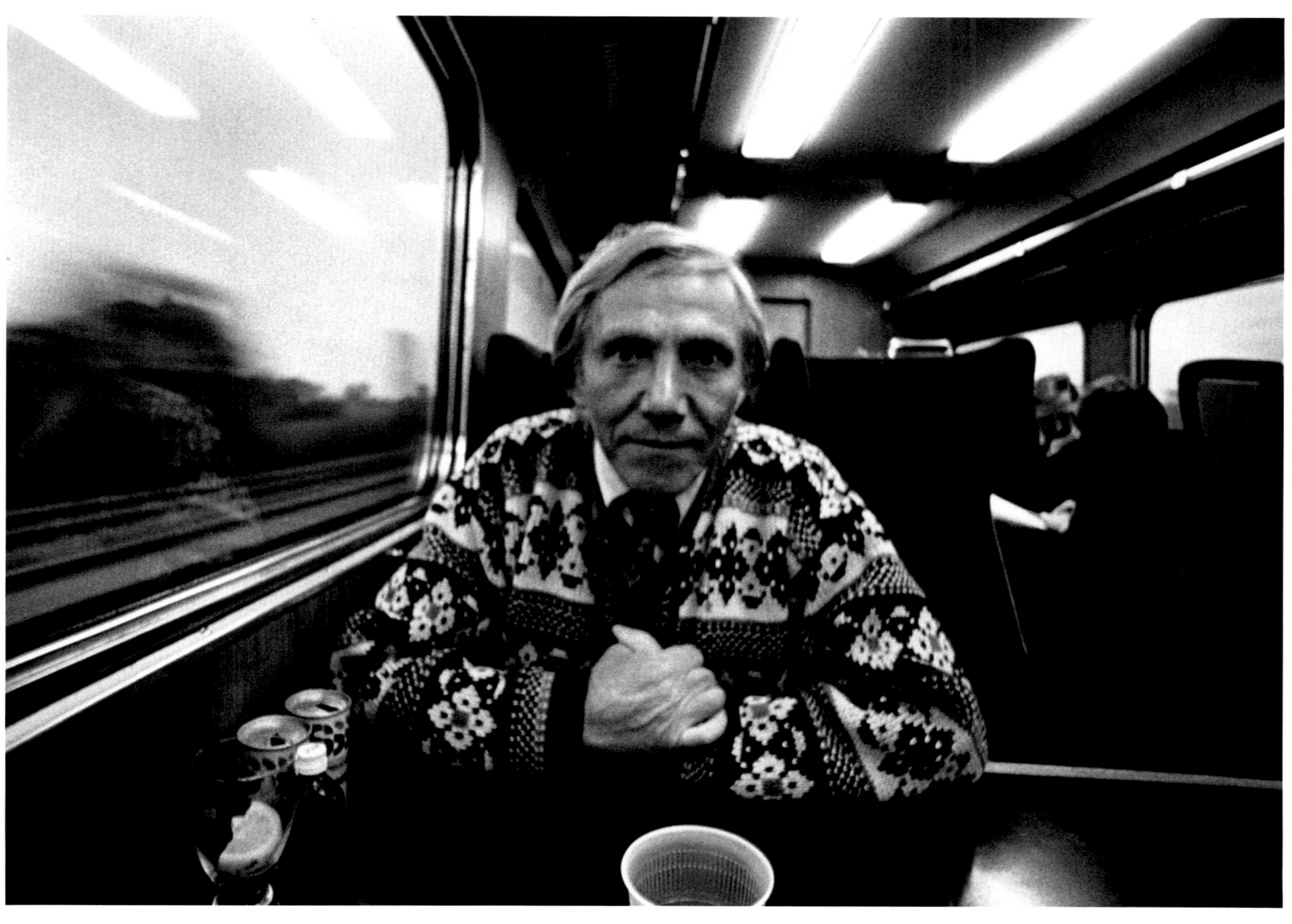

Harry from Australia   1978

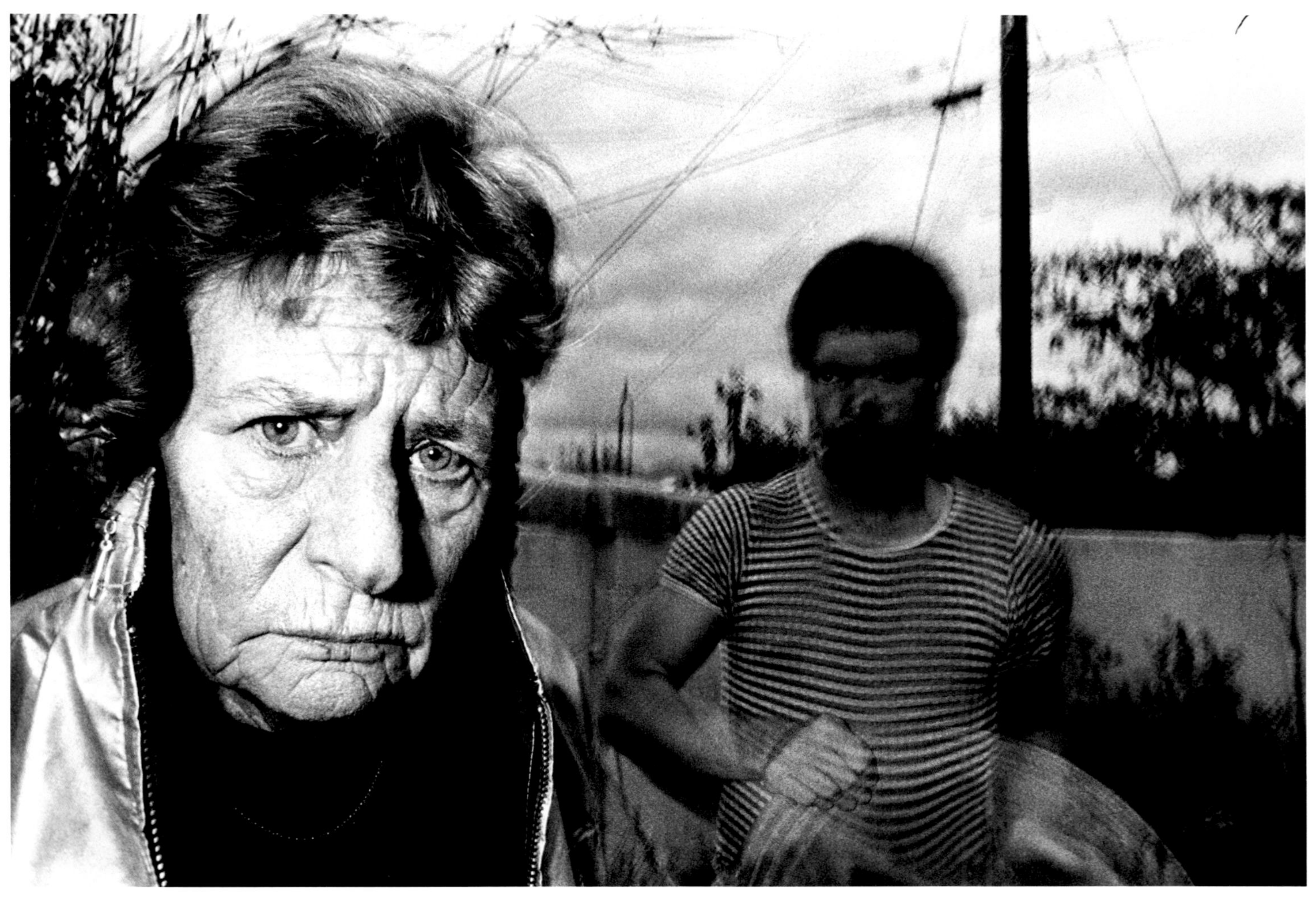

Shelley   1978

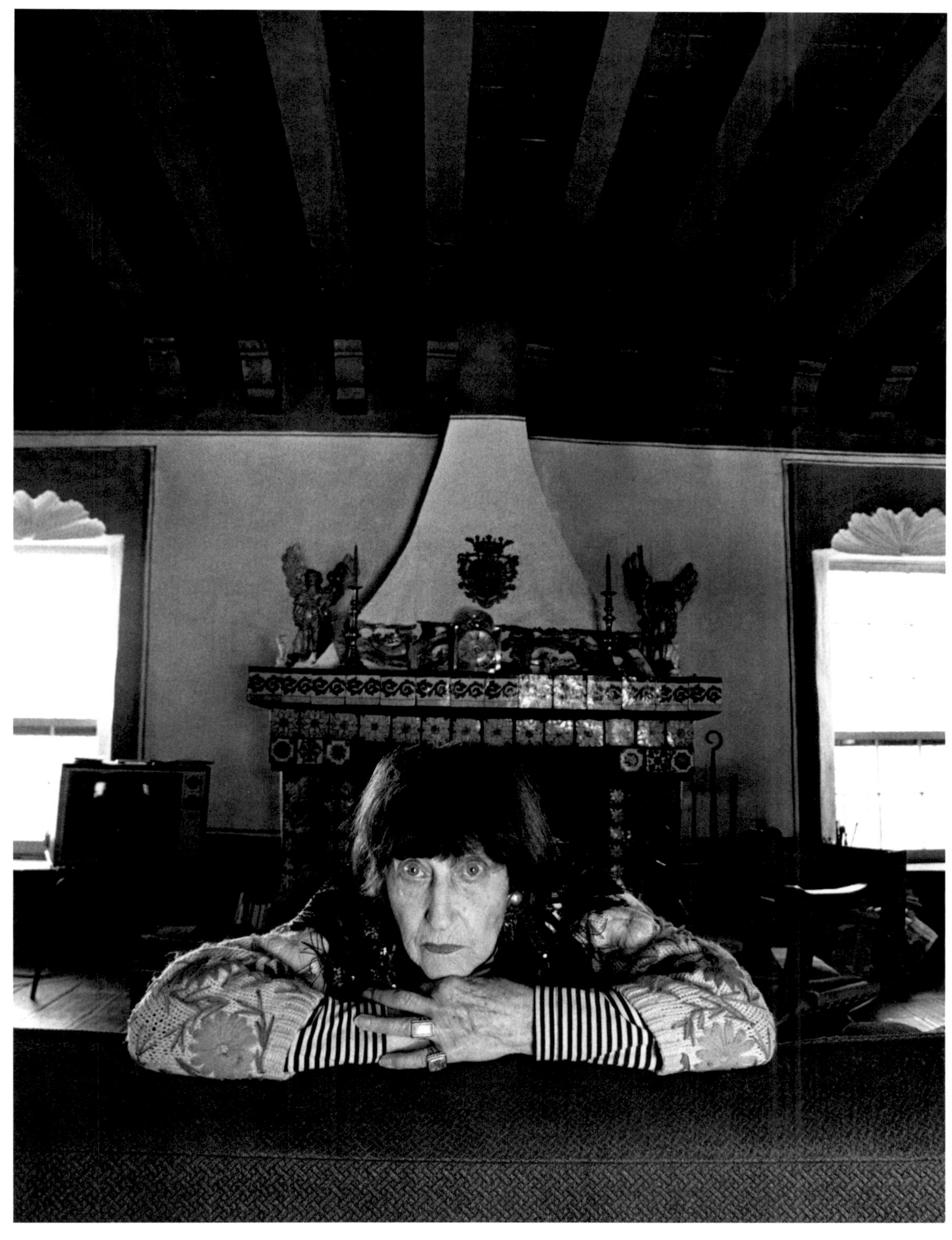

Yolanda   1978

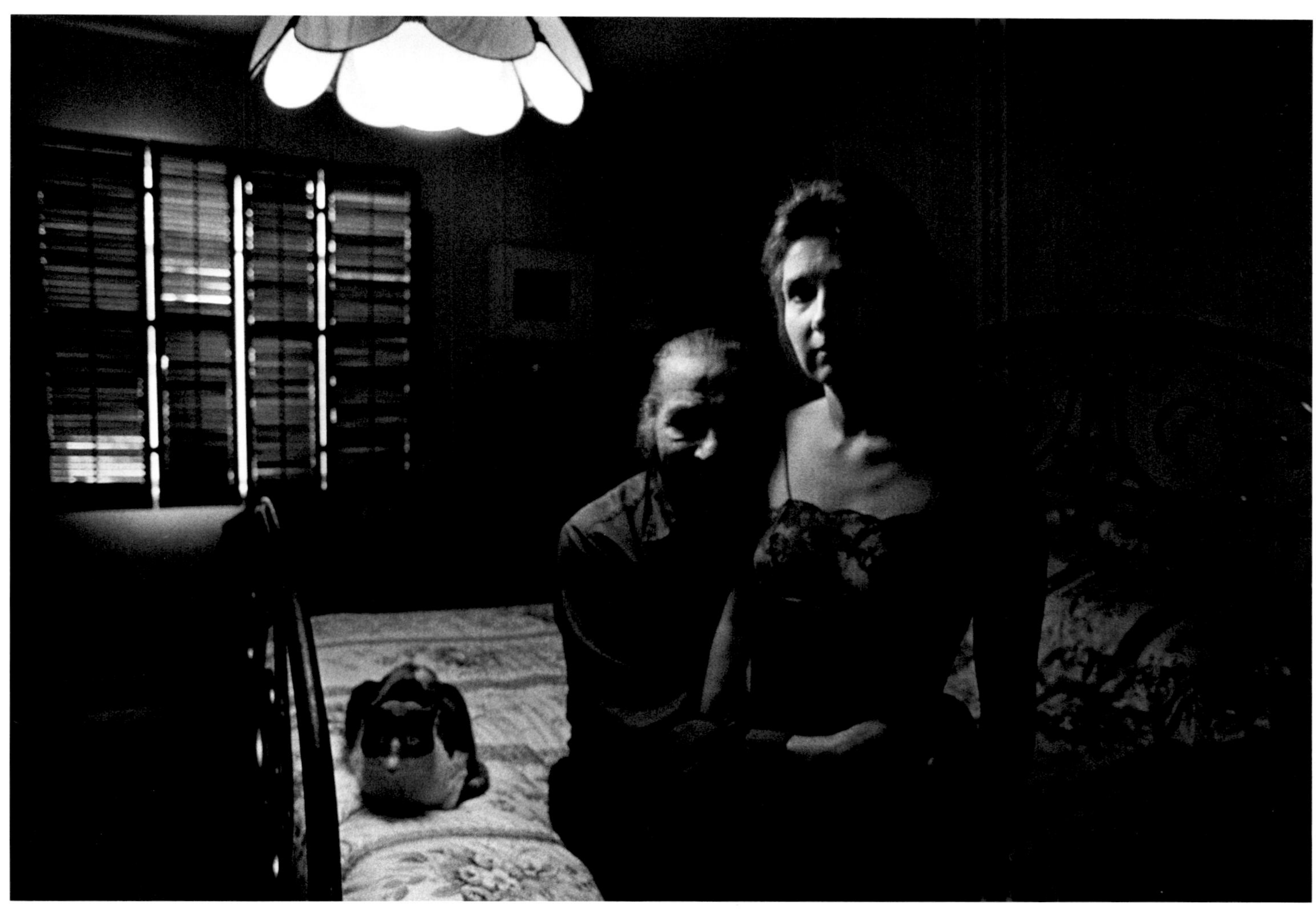

Silver Lining No. 1   1979

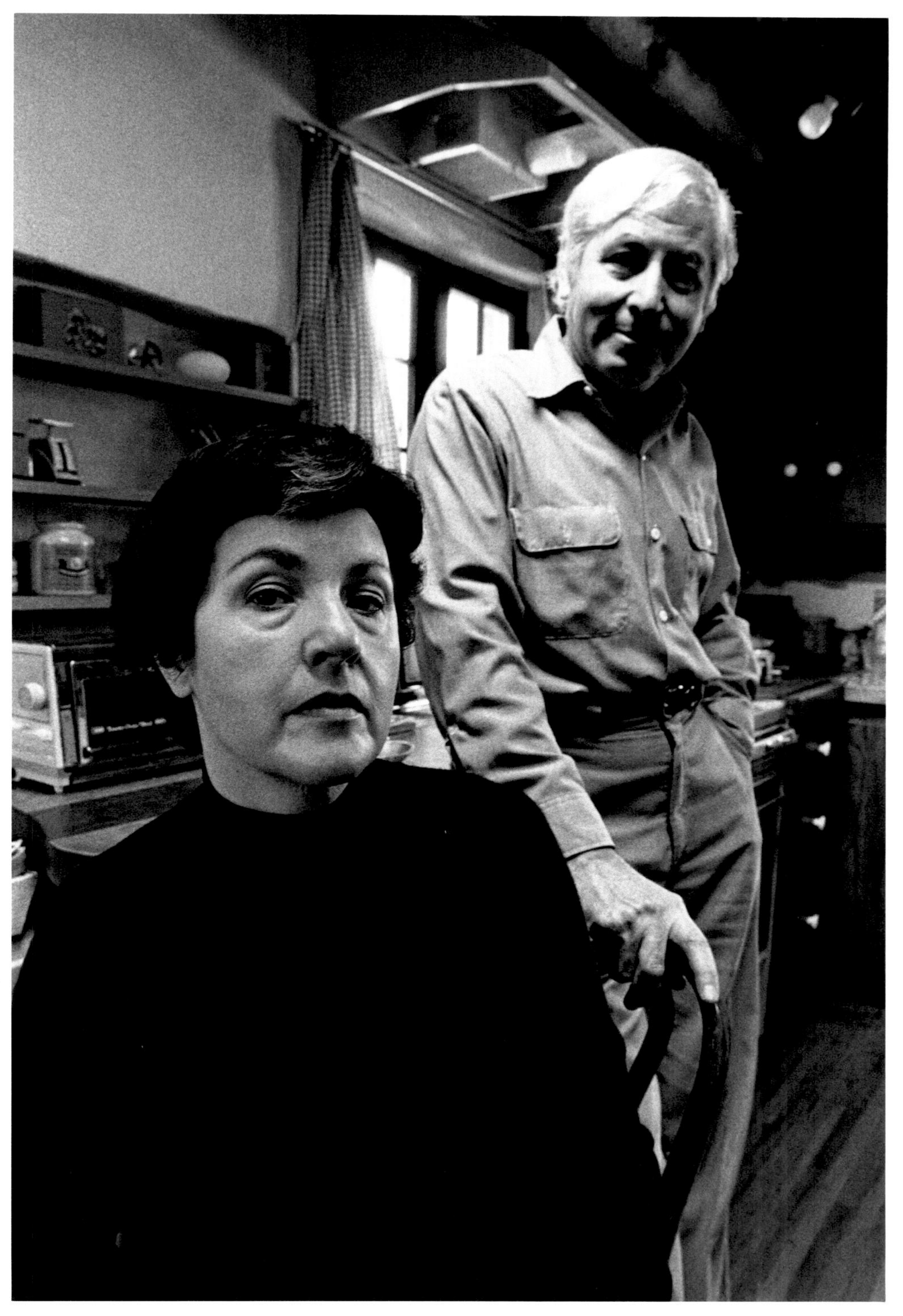

Silver Lining No. 2   1979

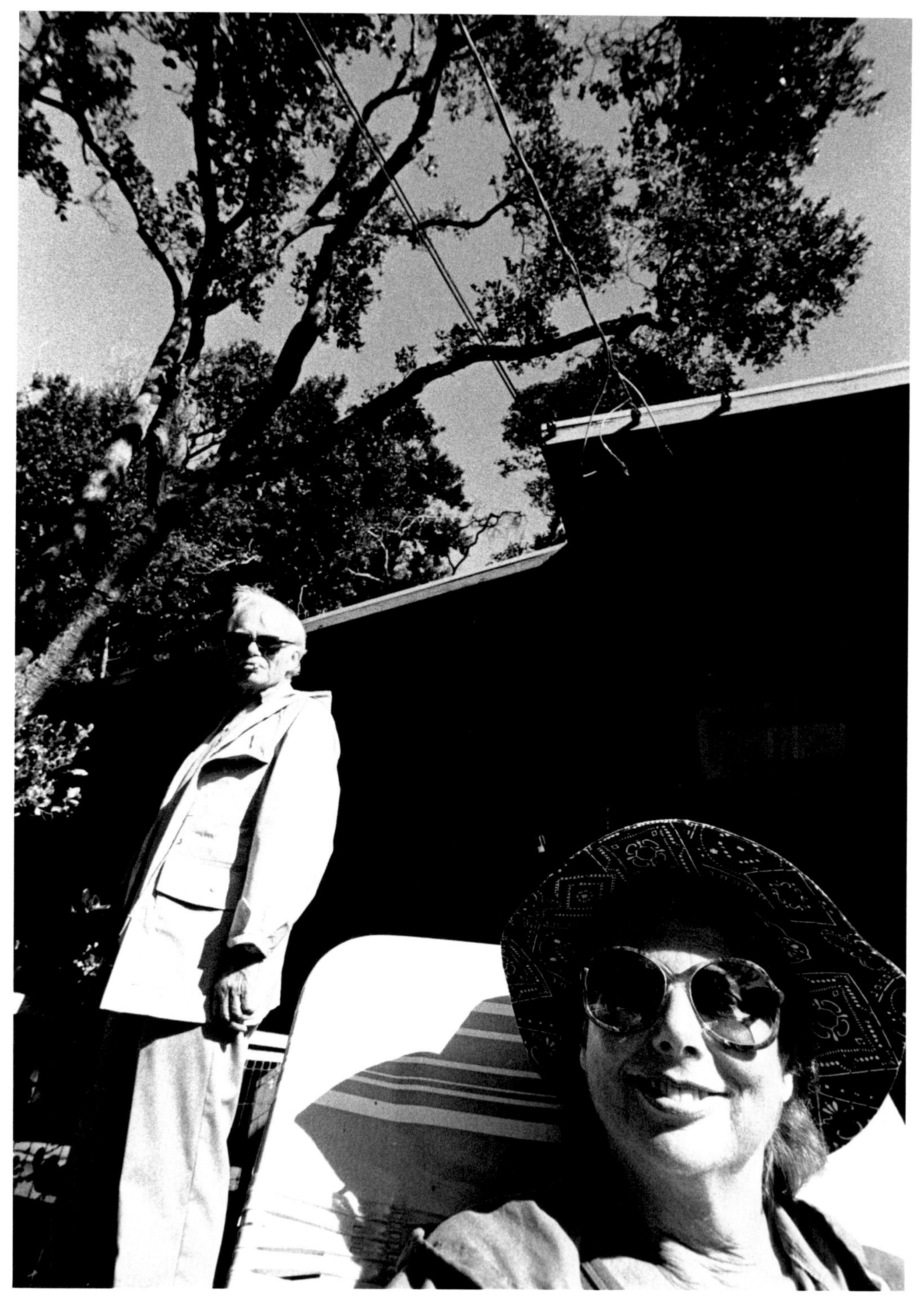

Silver Lining No. 3   1979

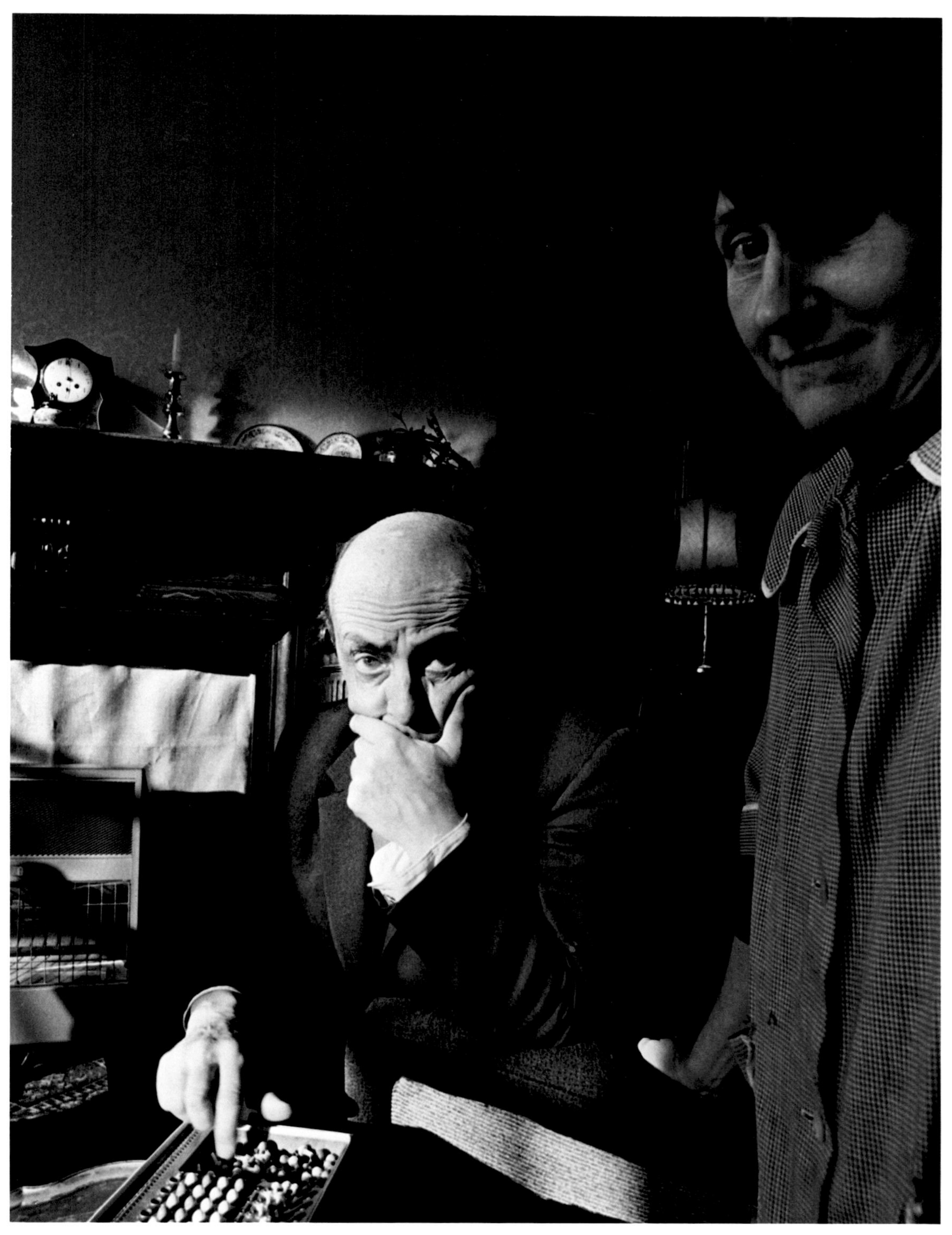

Silver Lining No. 4   1978

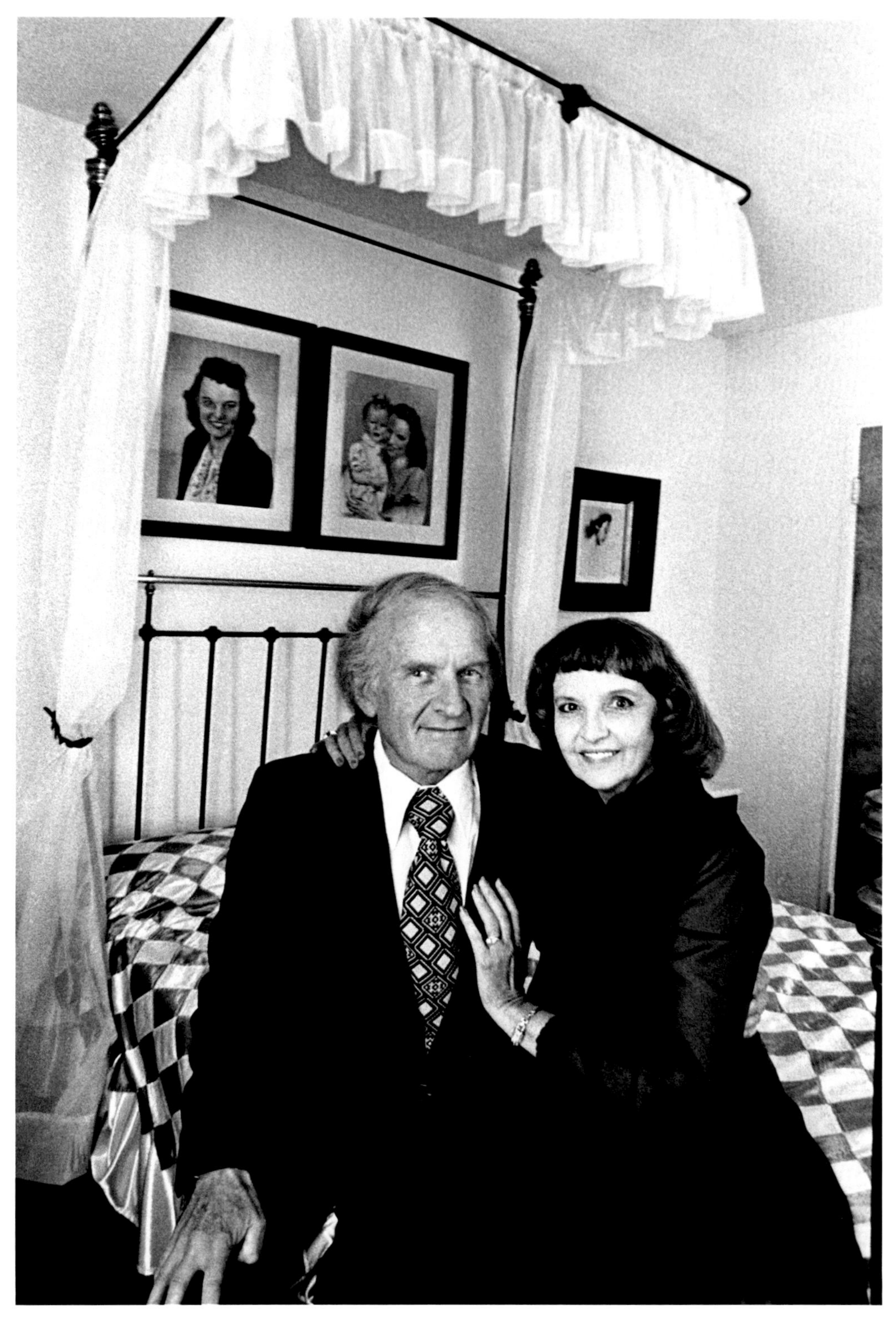

Silver Lining No. 5   1979

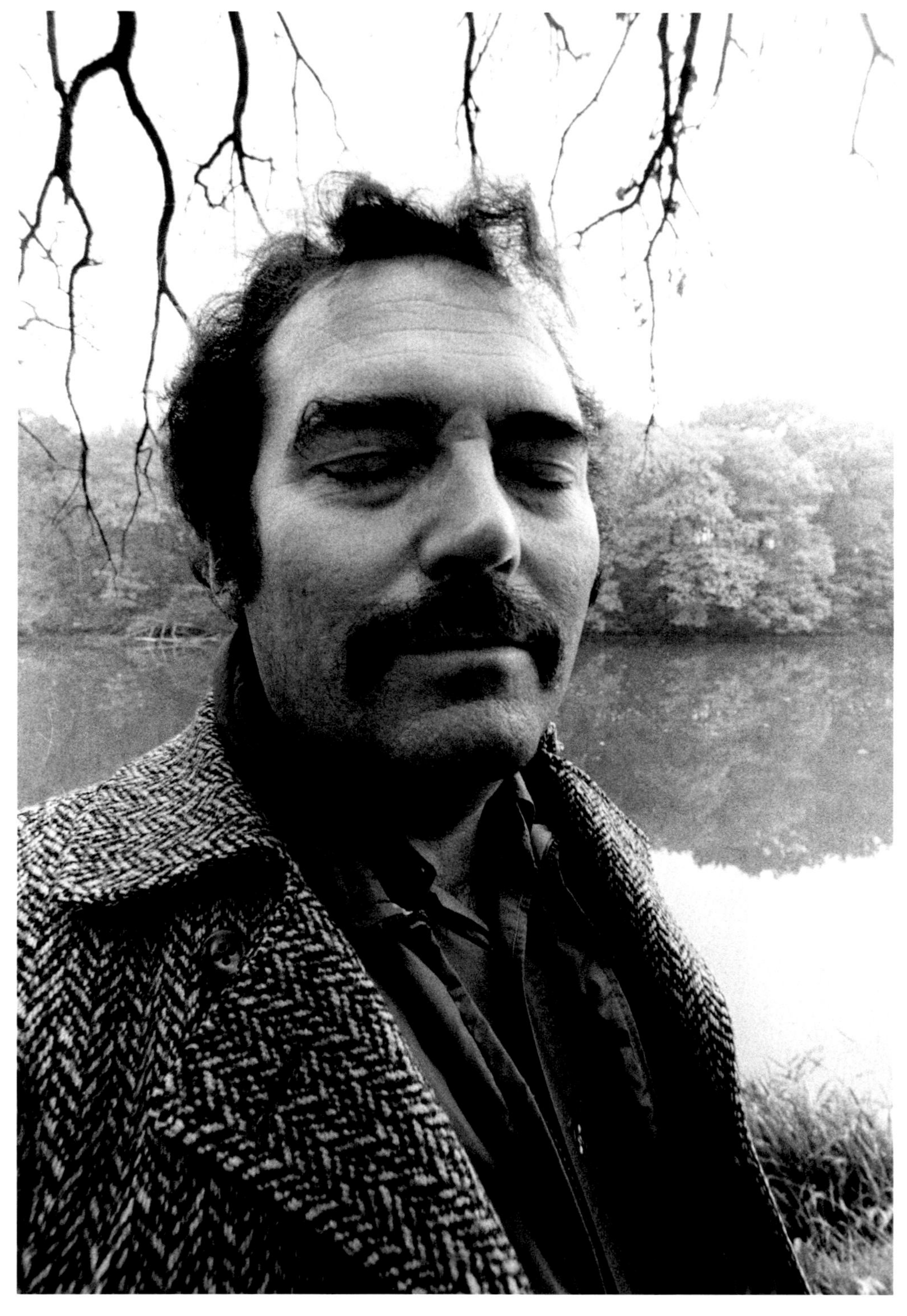

Cavalliere   1979

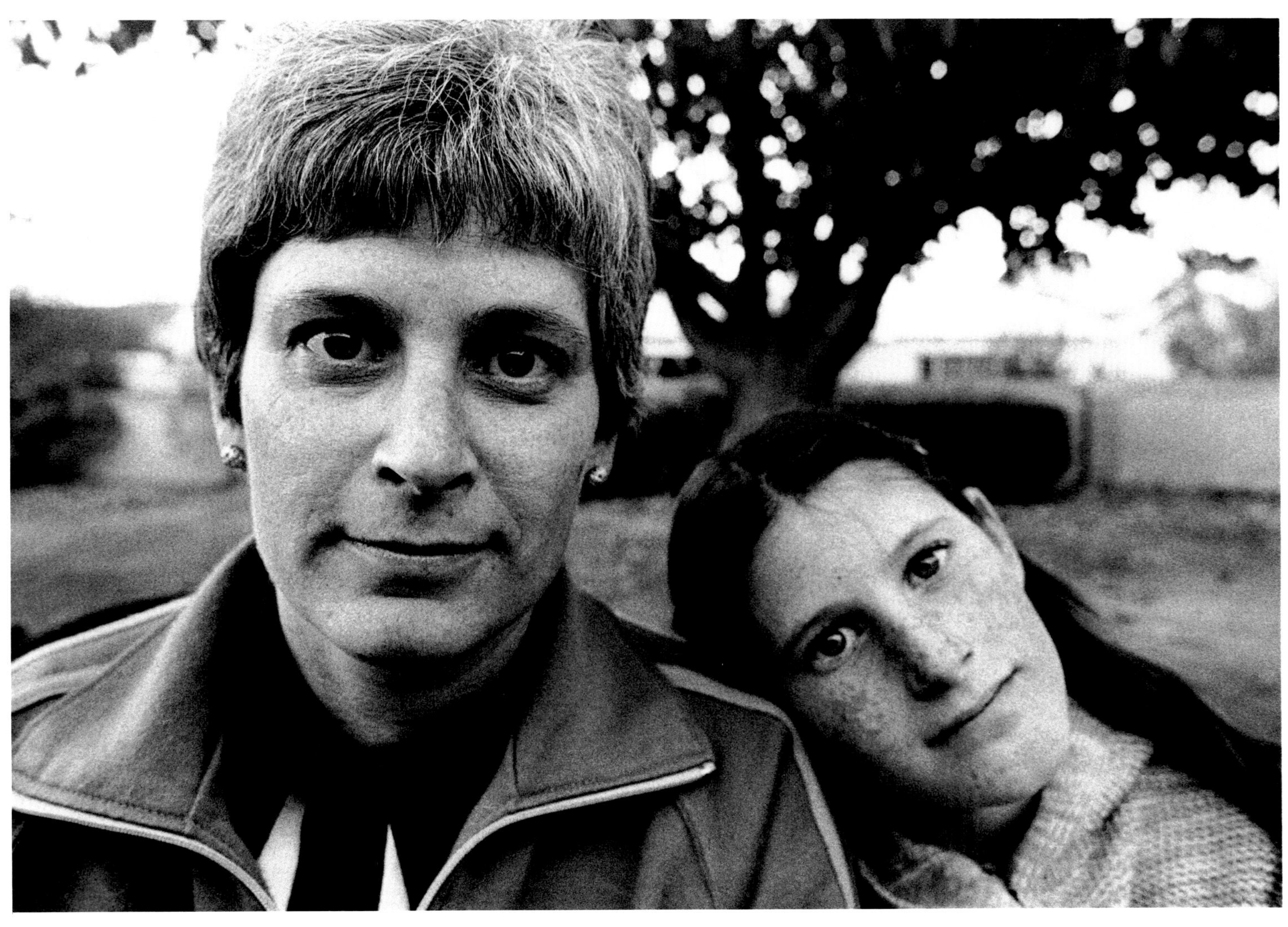

The Gay Divorcee   1979

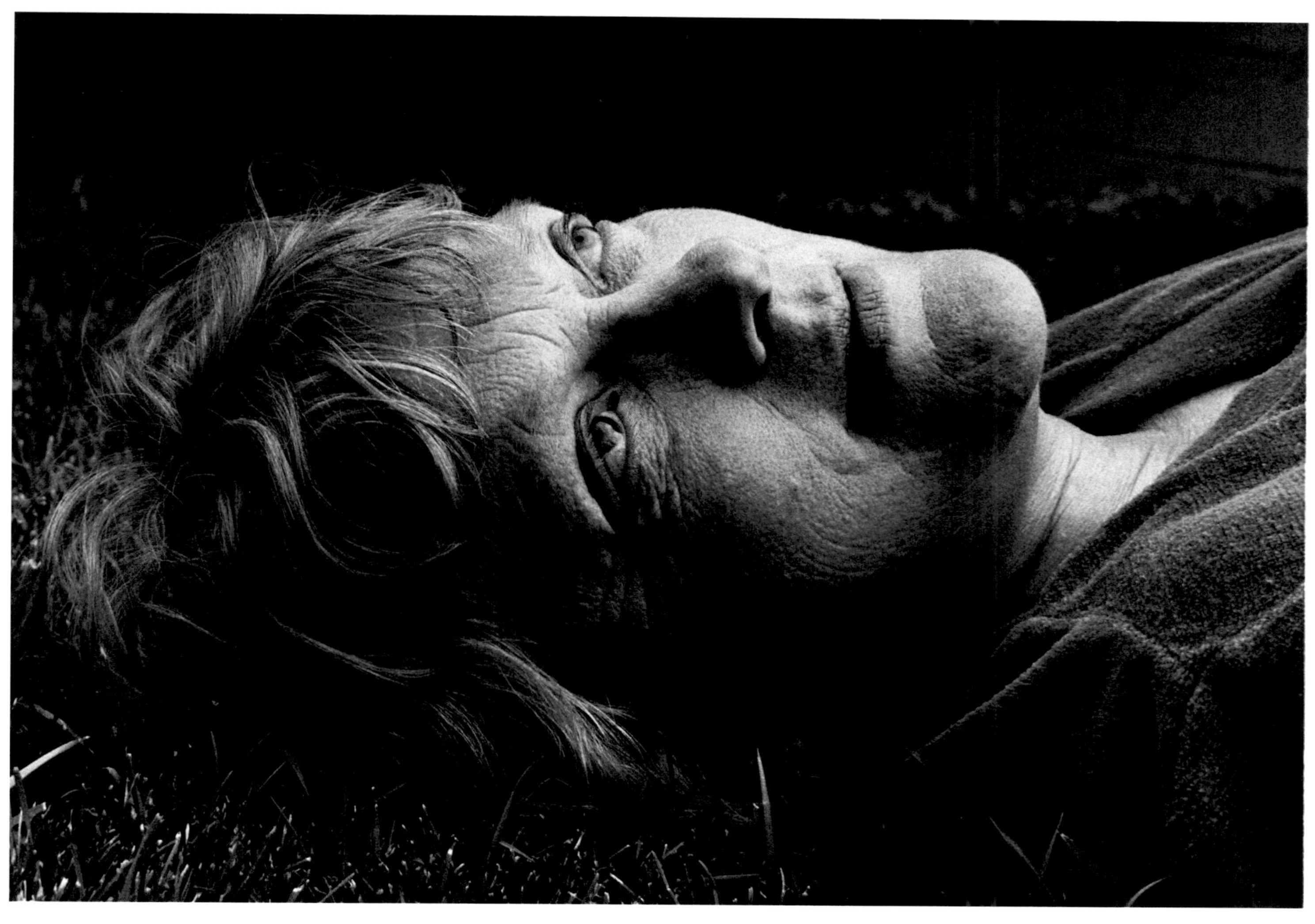

Self-image in the Grass   1979

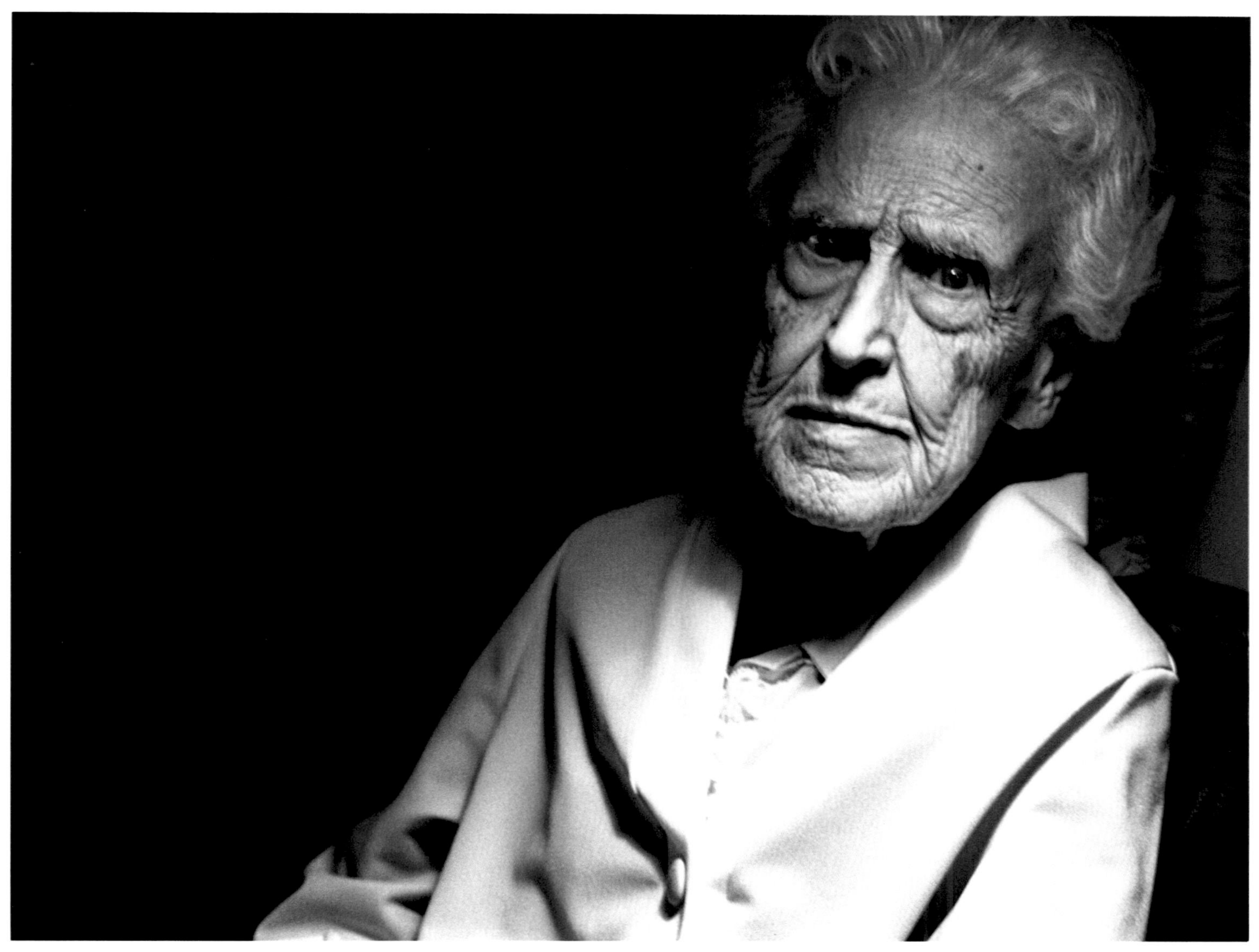

Agnes   1979

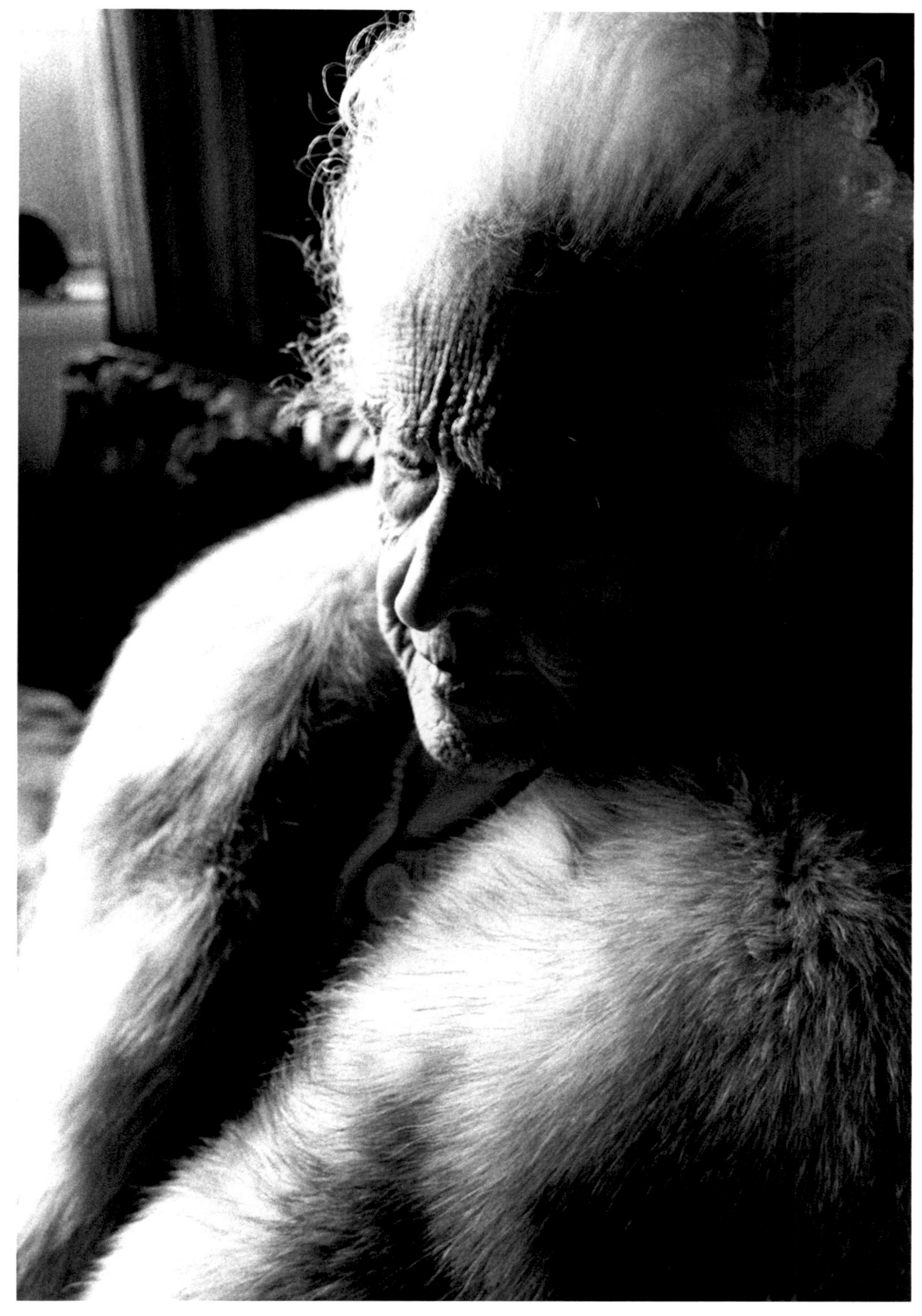

Agnes in a Fur Collar   1979

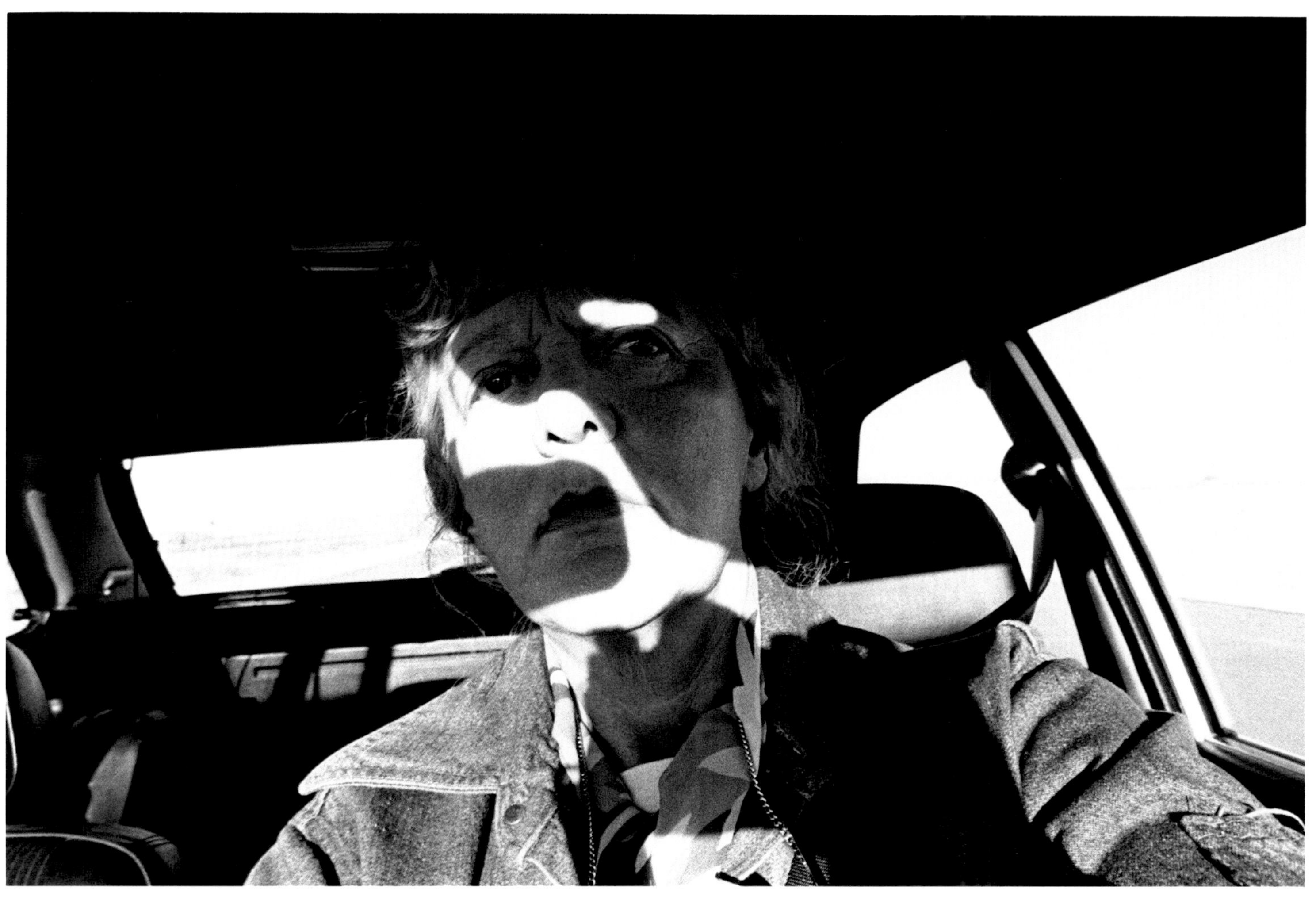

Self-image   1979

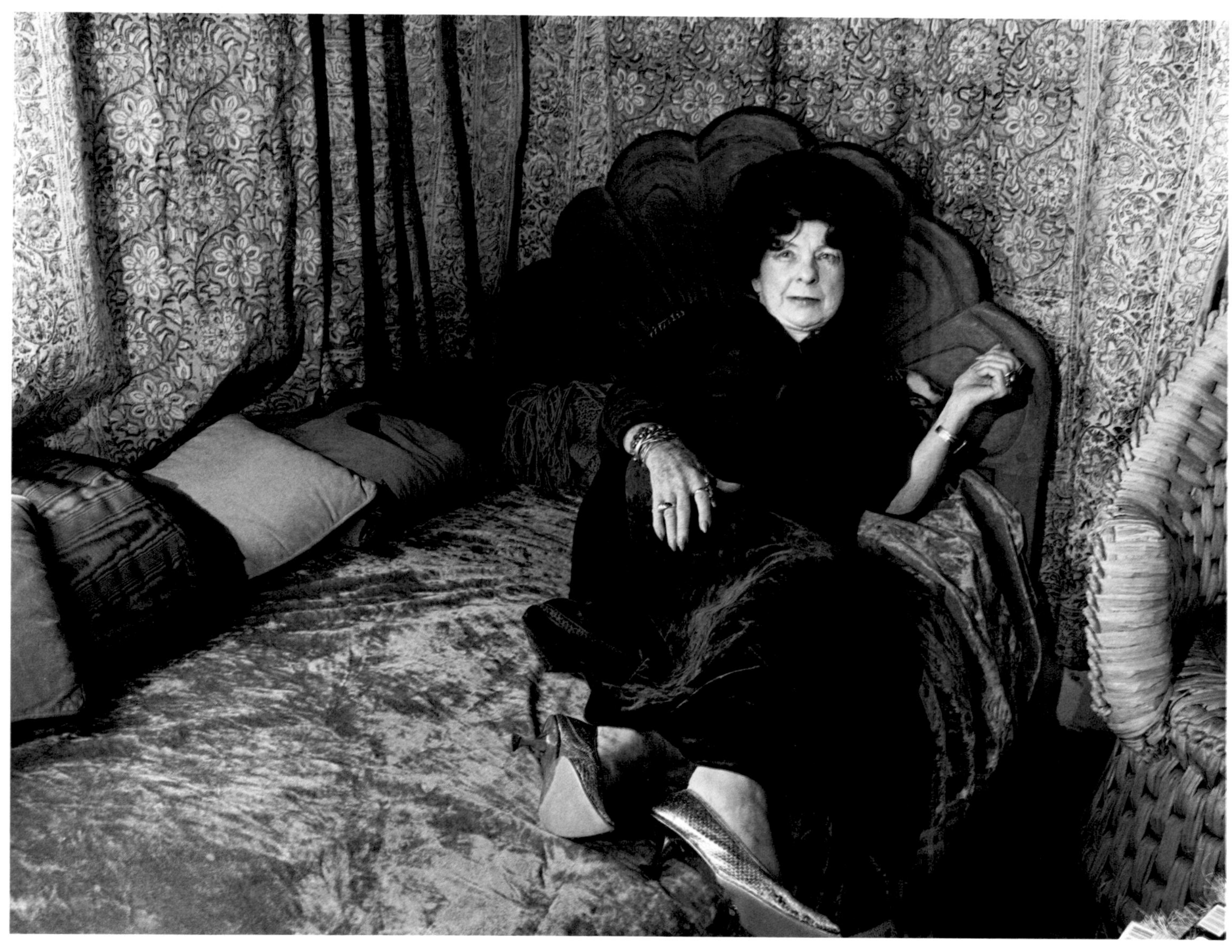

Ruth Leakey   1980

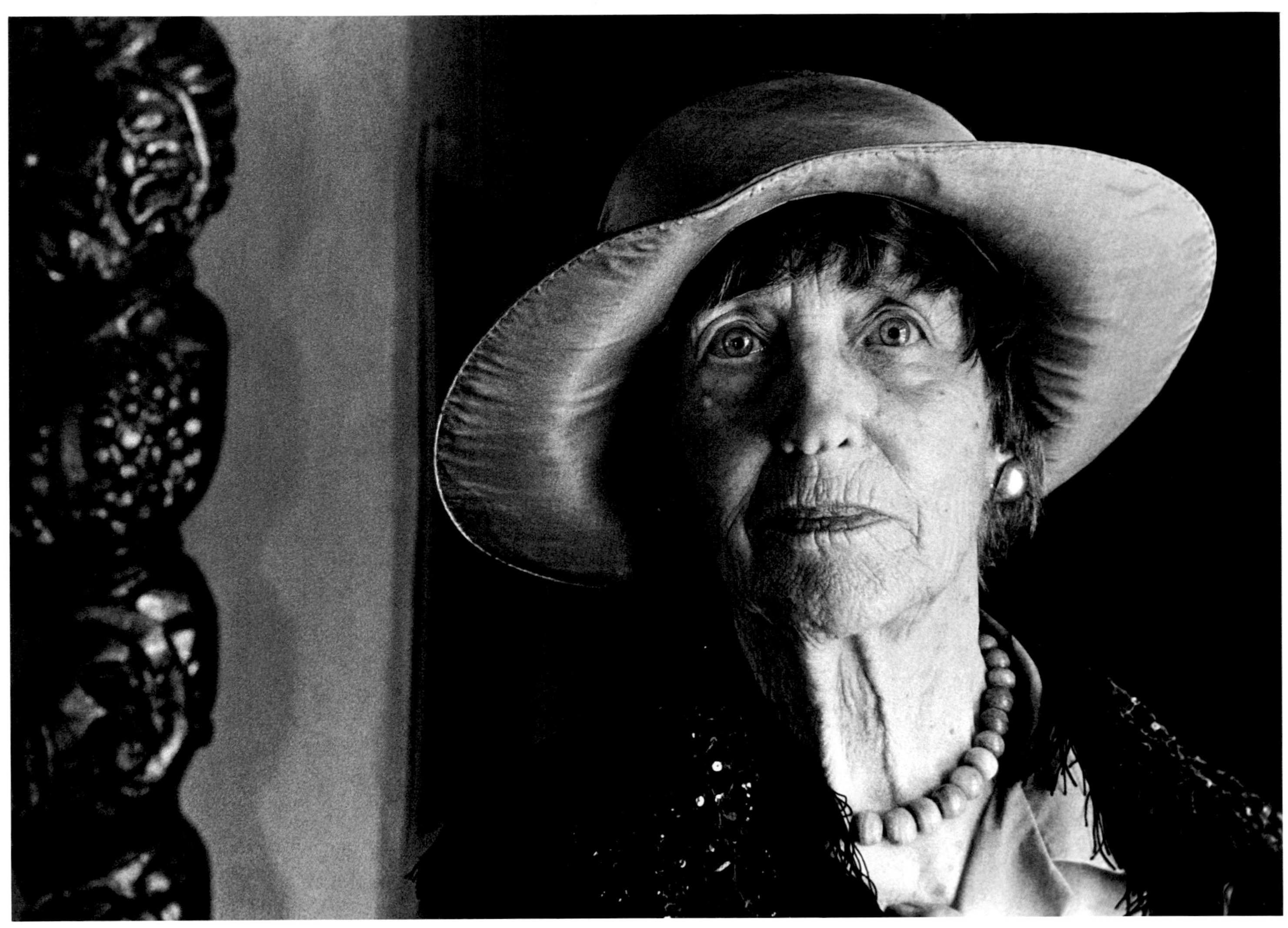

Yolanda in Her Silk Hat   1980

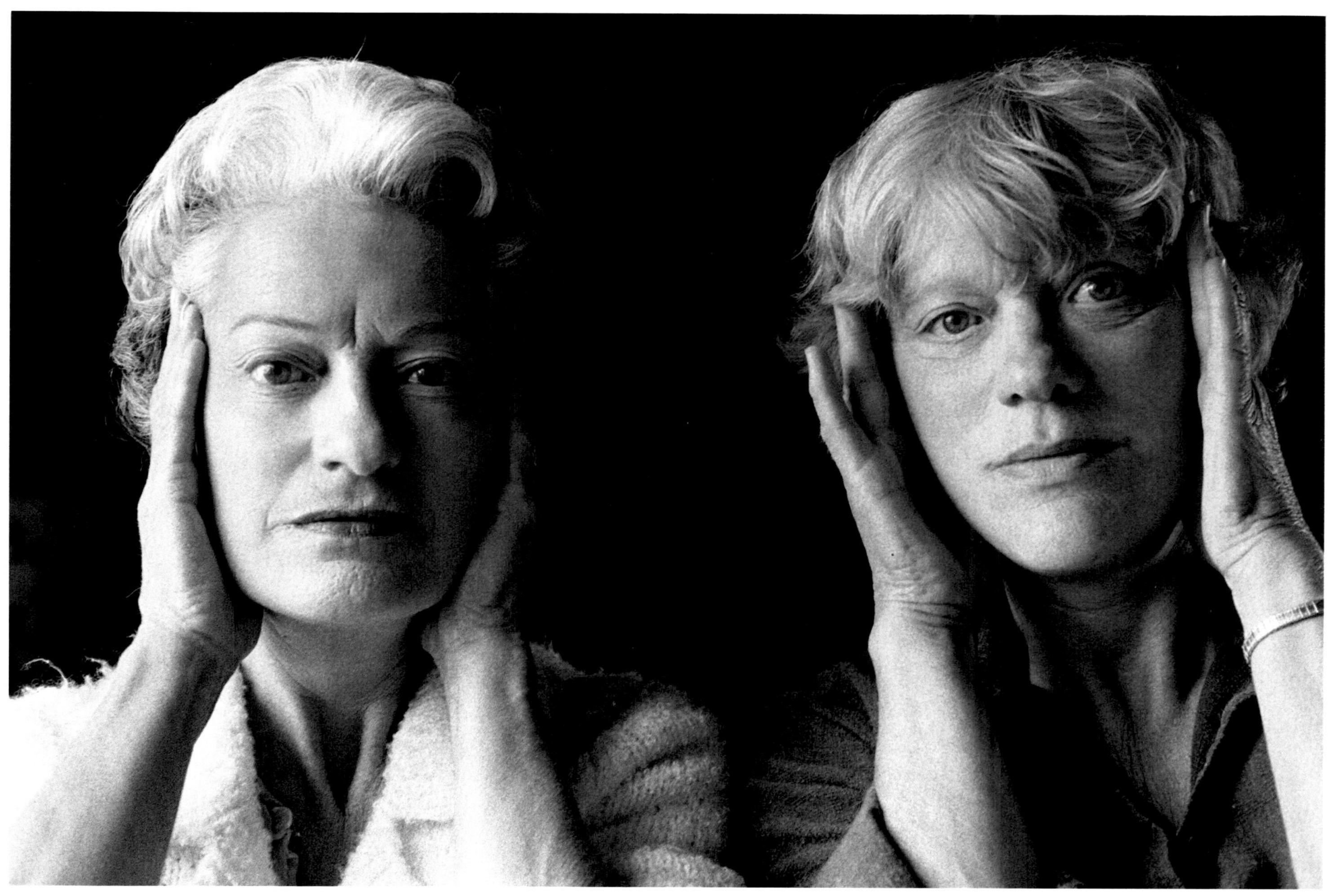

Reminiscence: Portrait with My Sister   1980

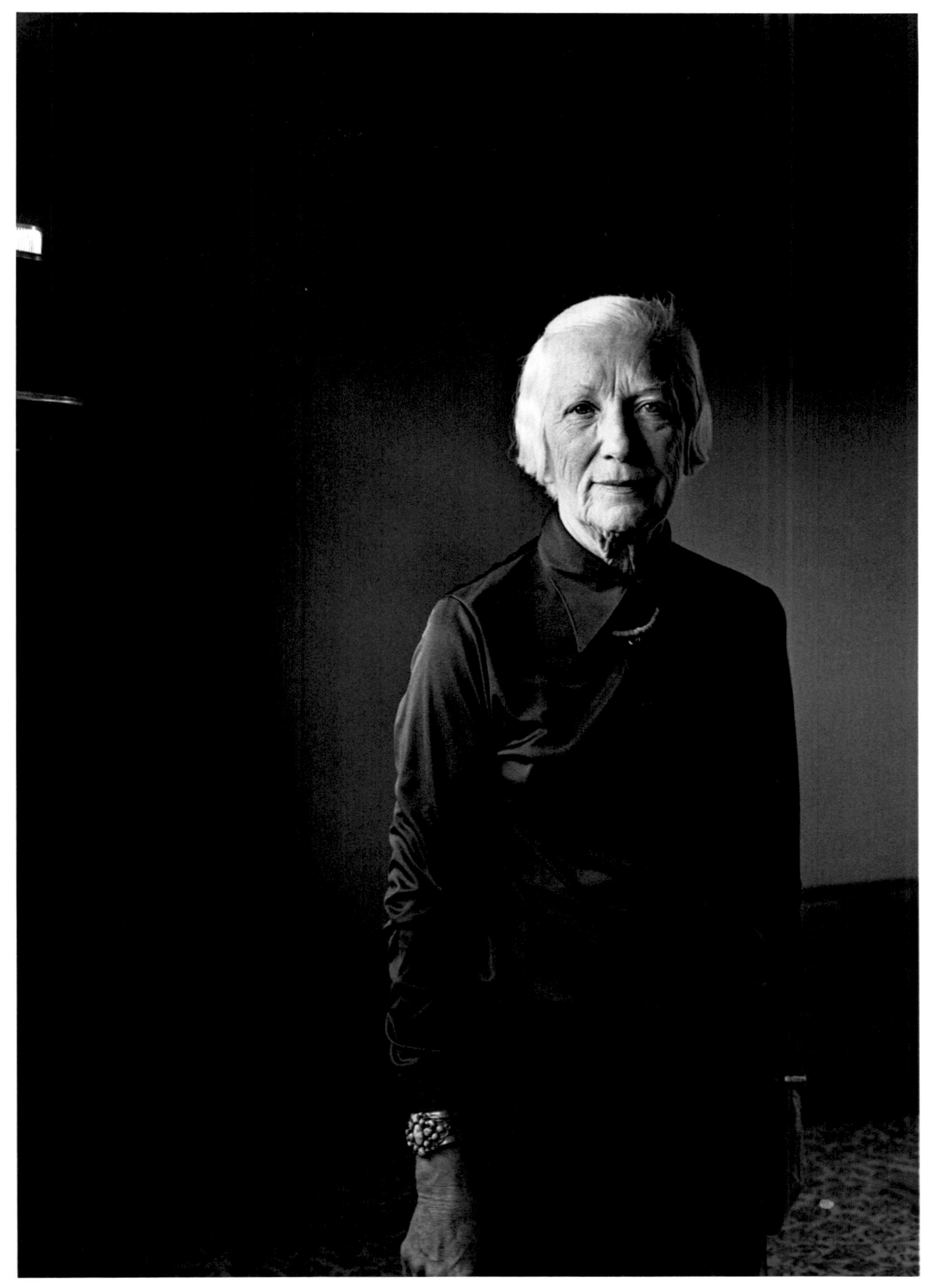

Mary Jenkins   1980

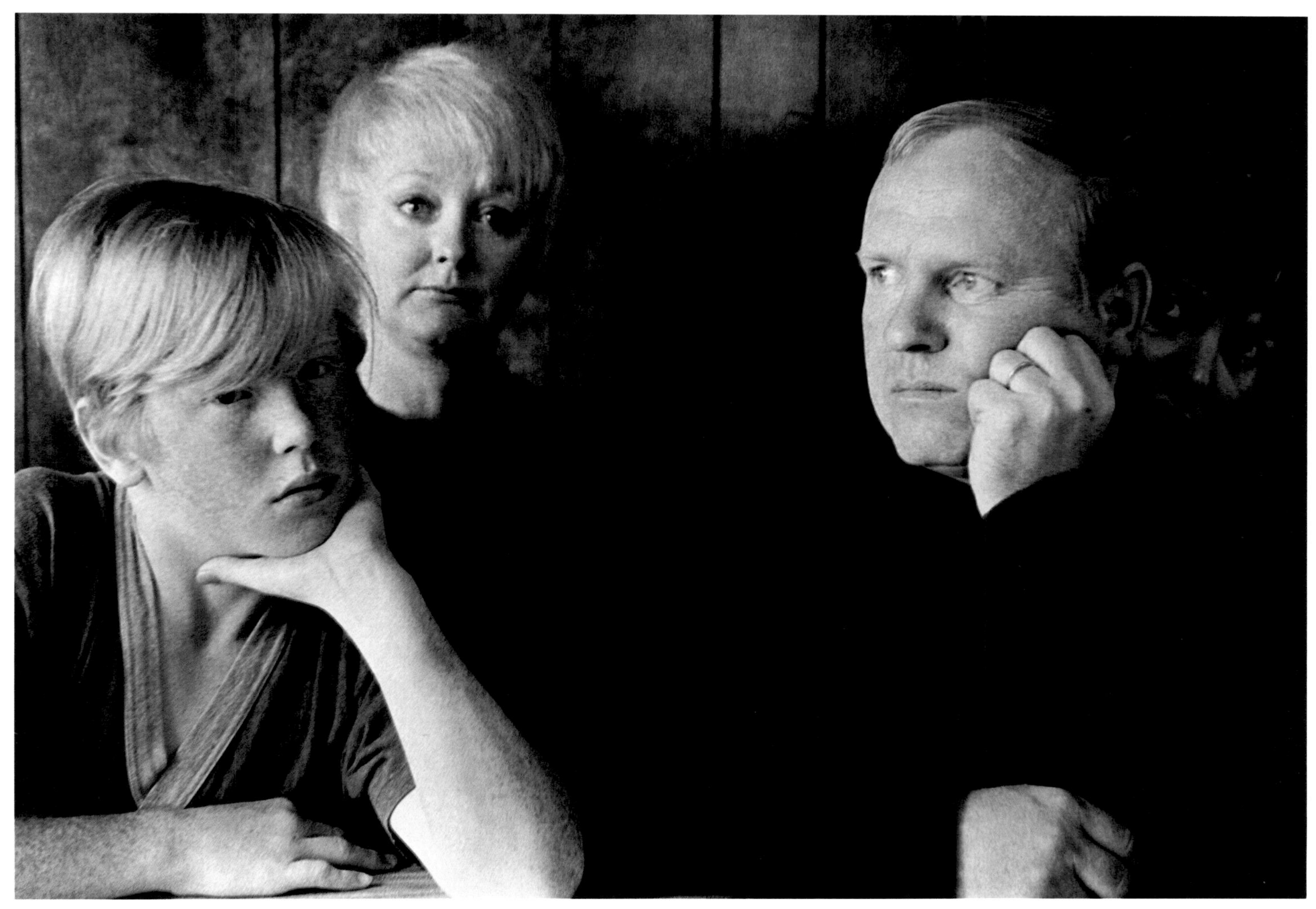

A Family Portrait, Bellingham, Washington   1981

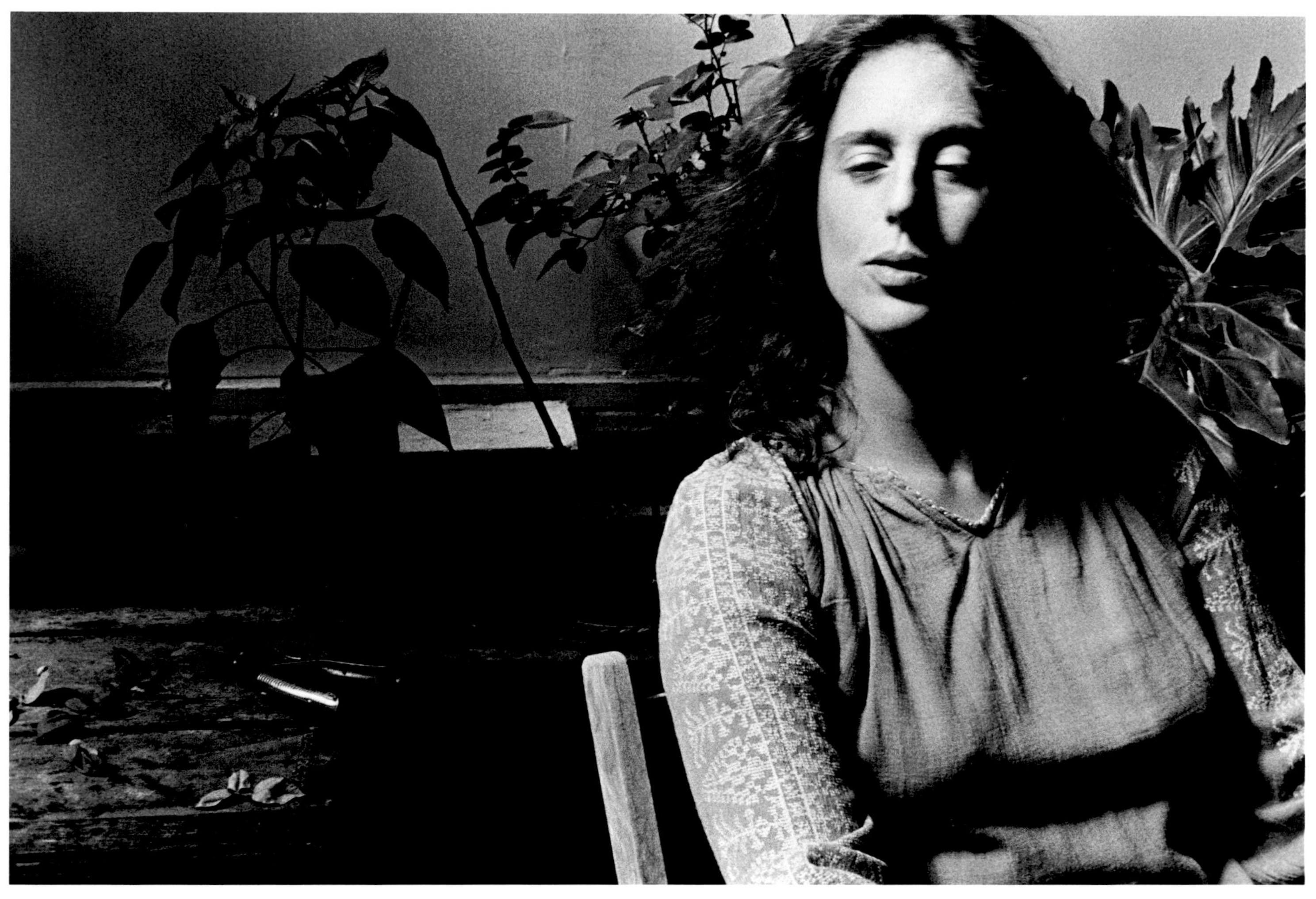

Louise   1981

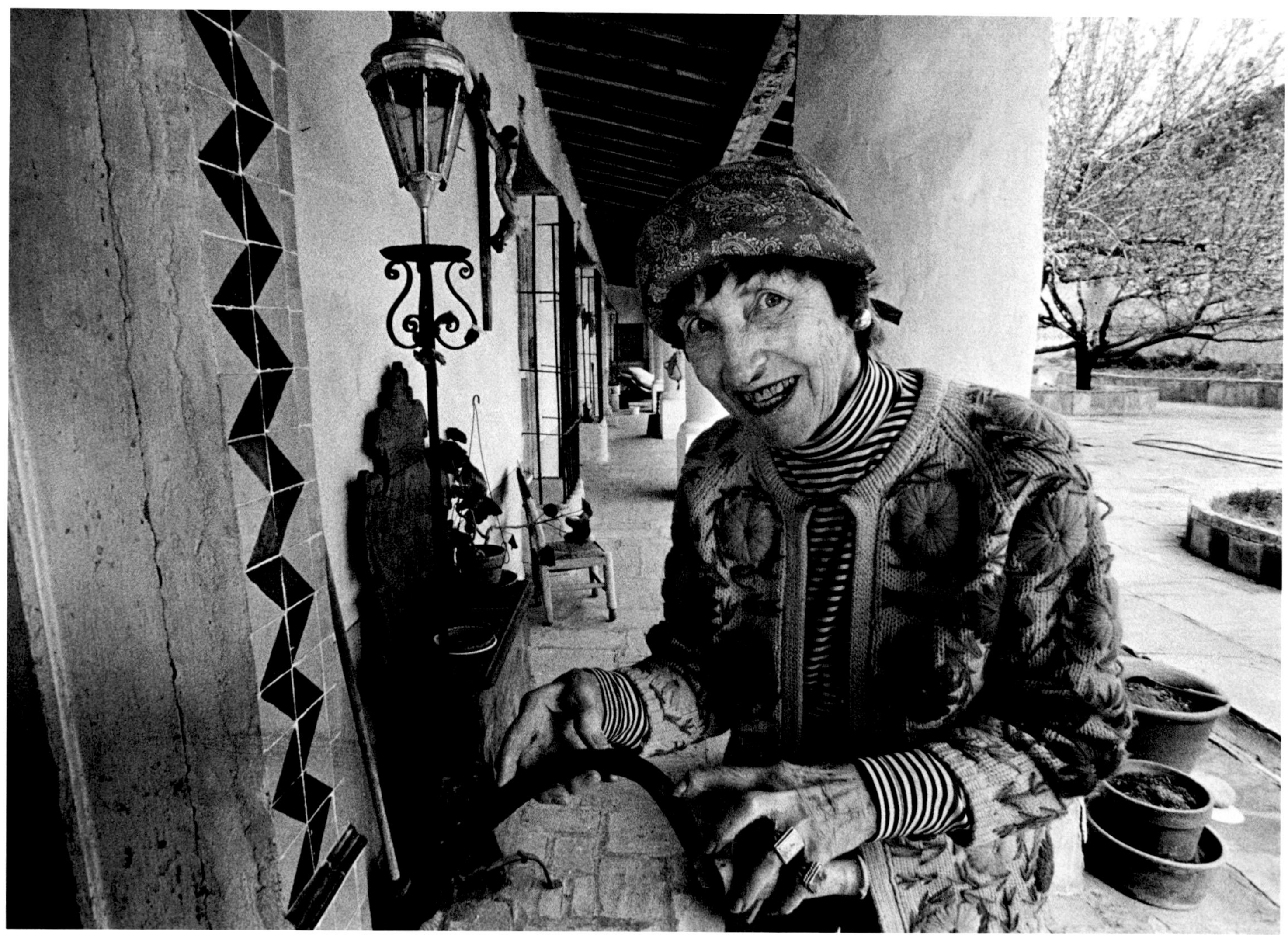

Yolanda in the Patio   1981

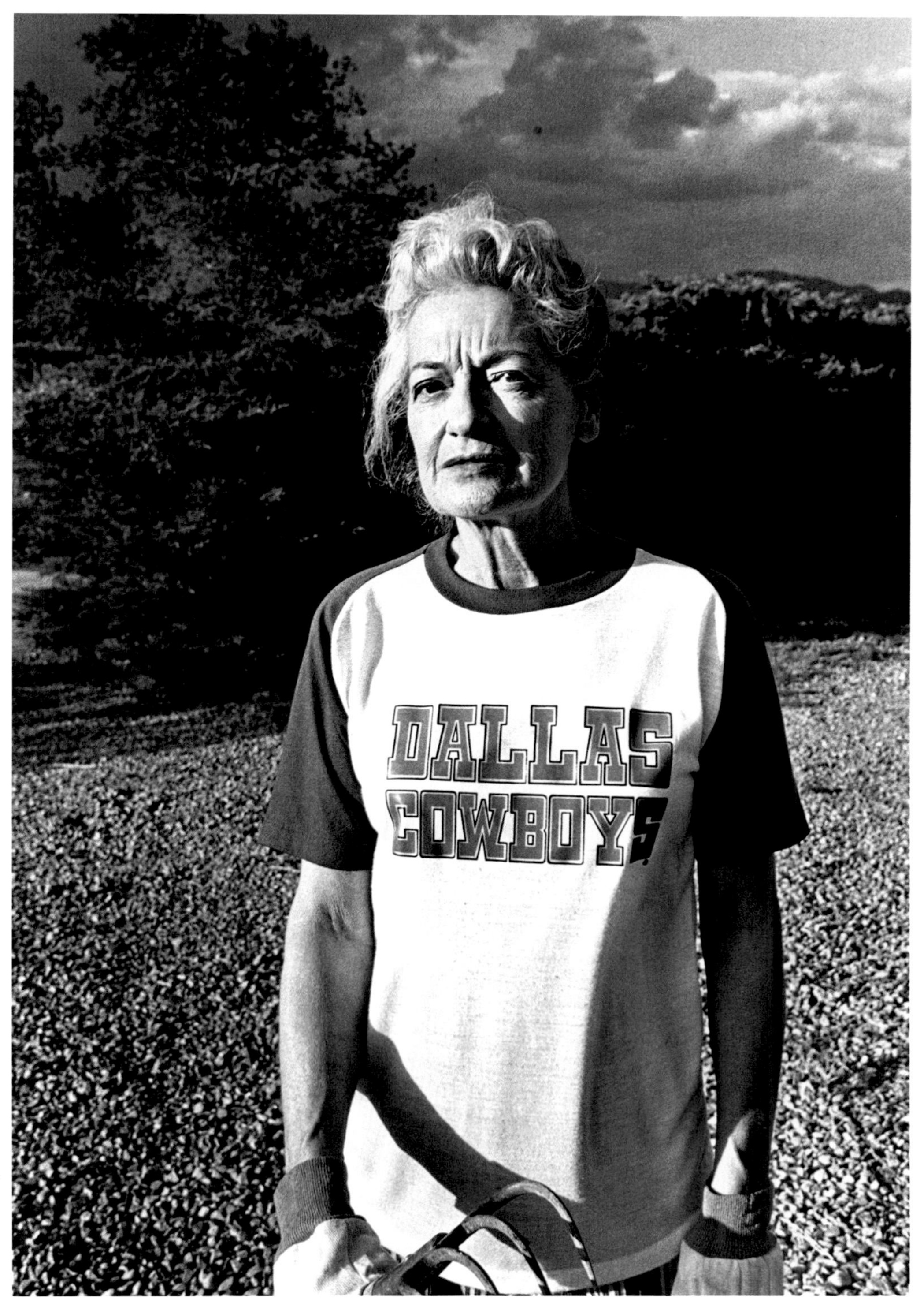

Mary   1981

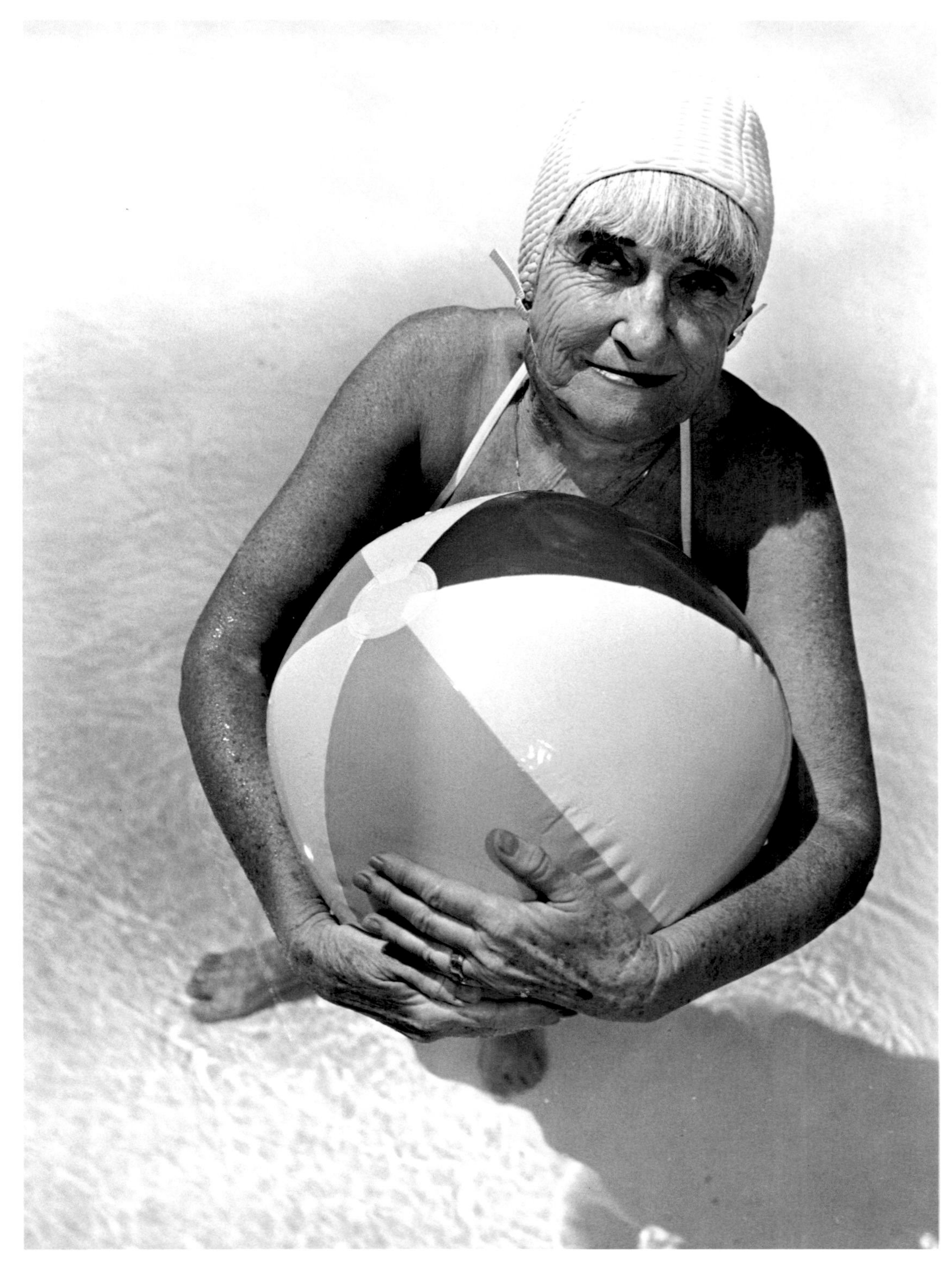

Edith "Tiny" Keene   1981

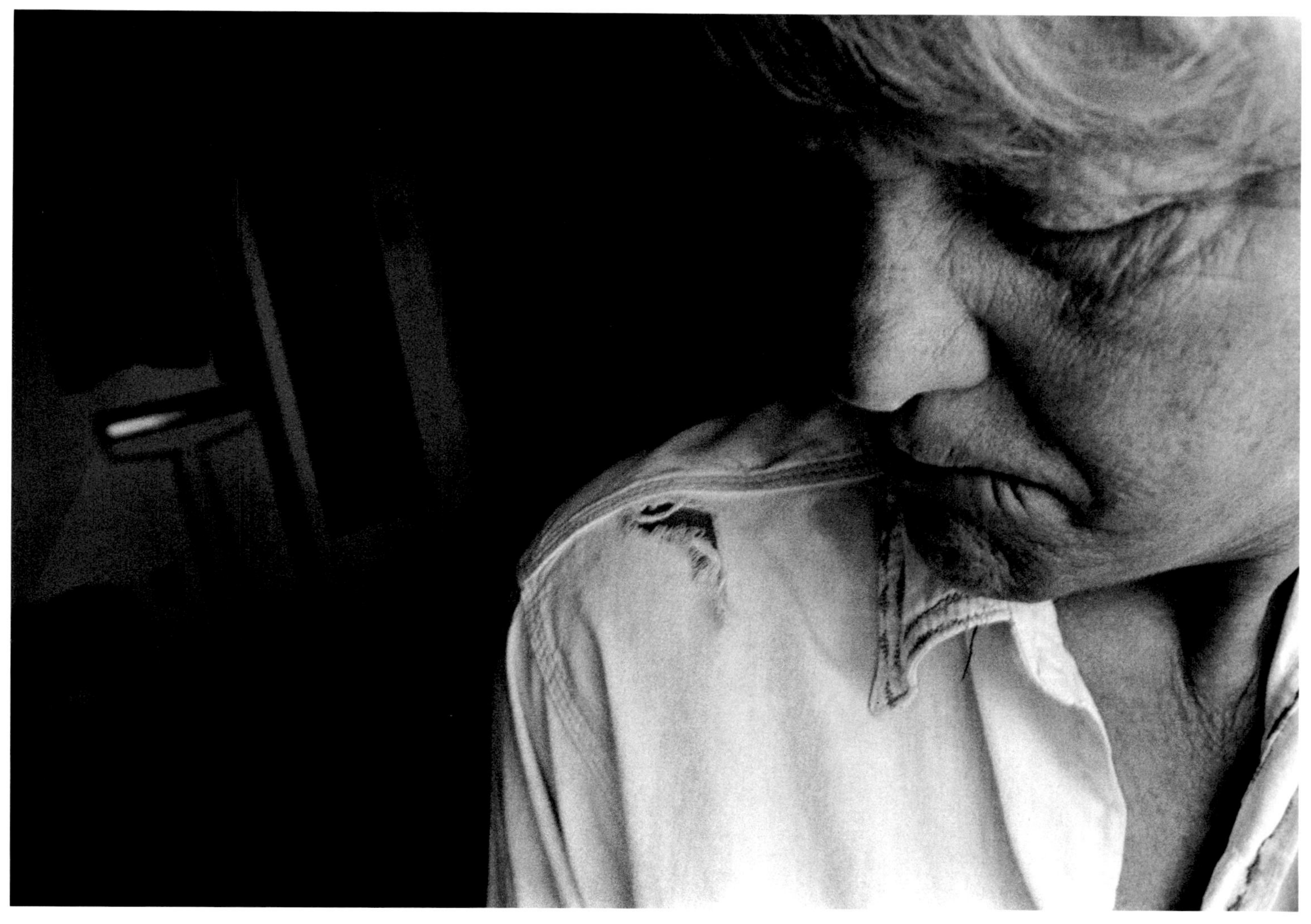

Darkroom   1981

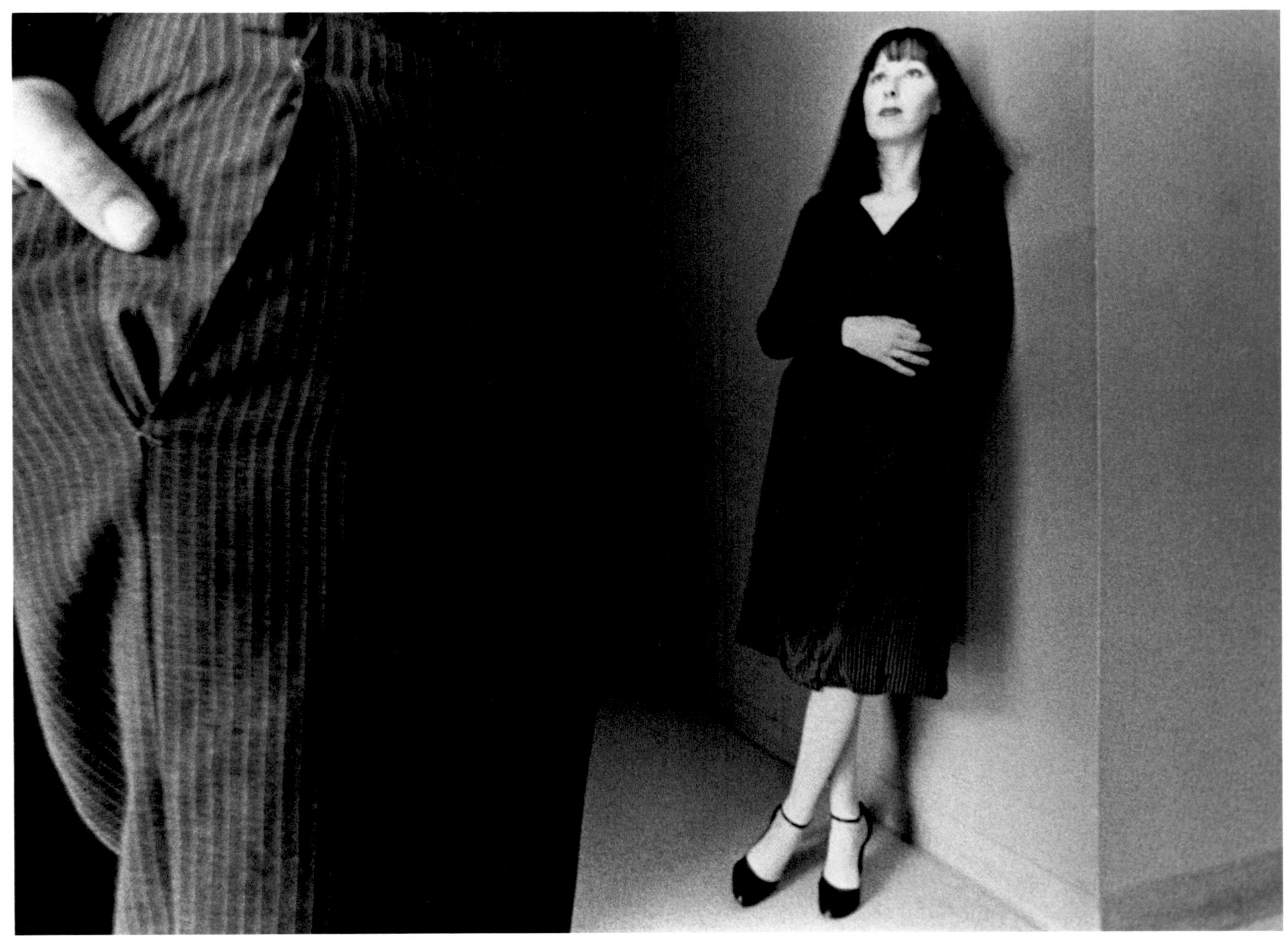

Untitled   1981

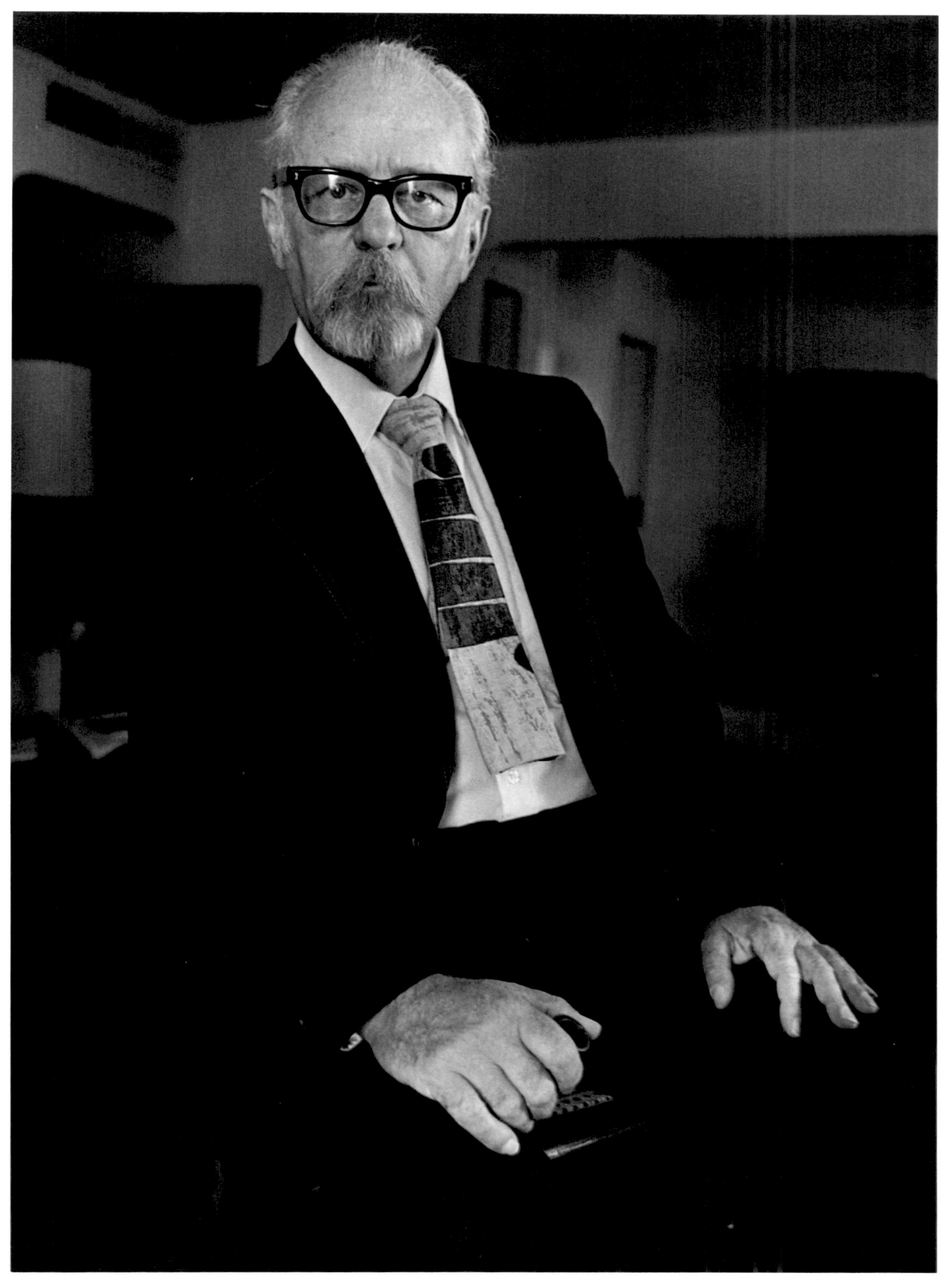

Henry Bumkin, Detective   1981

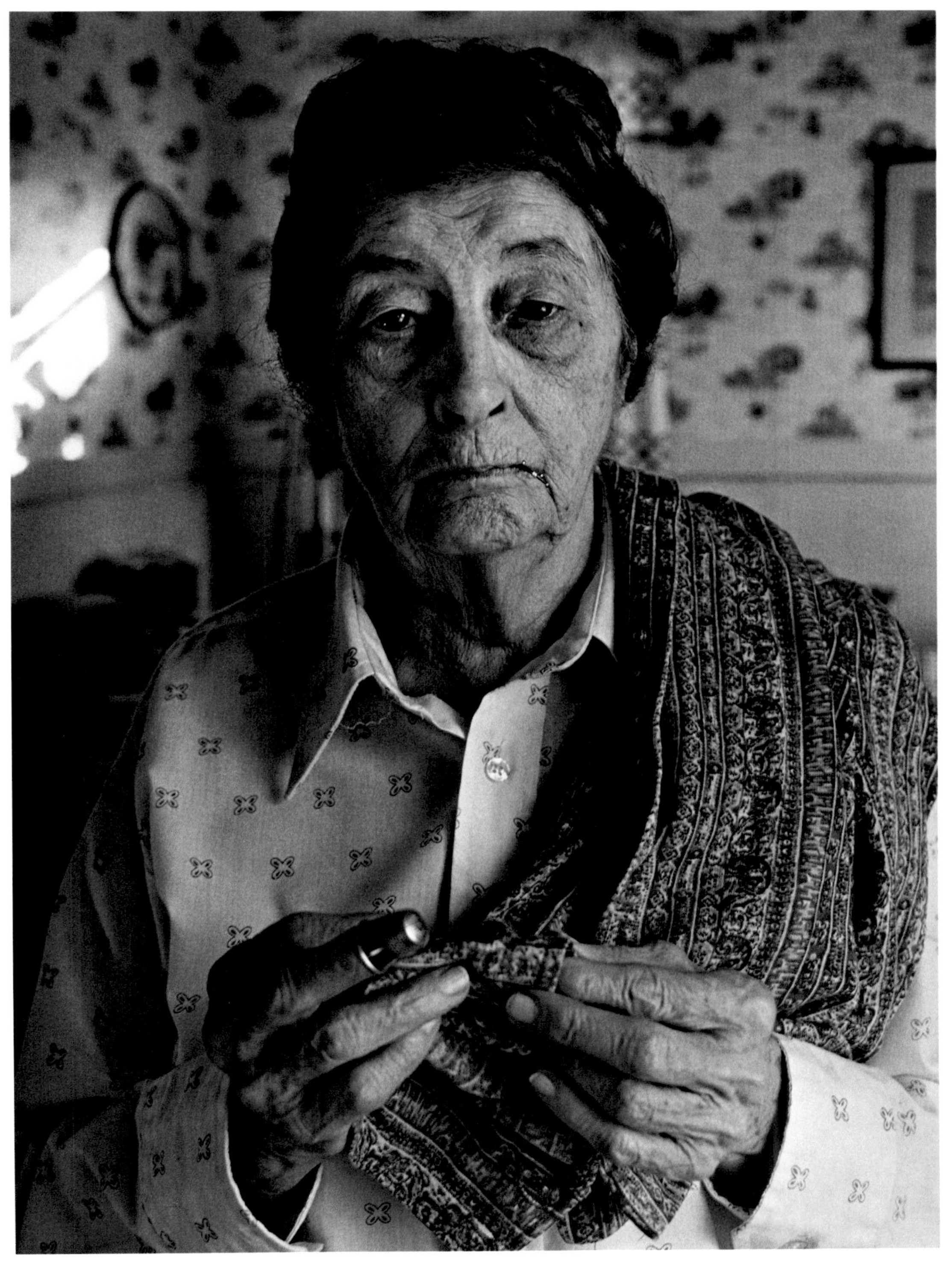

Rosa Wiley, Seamstress   1982

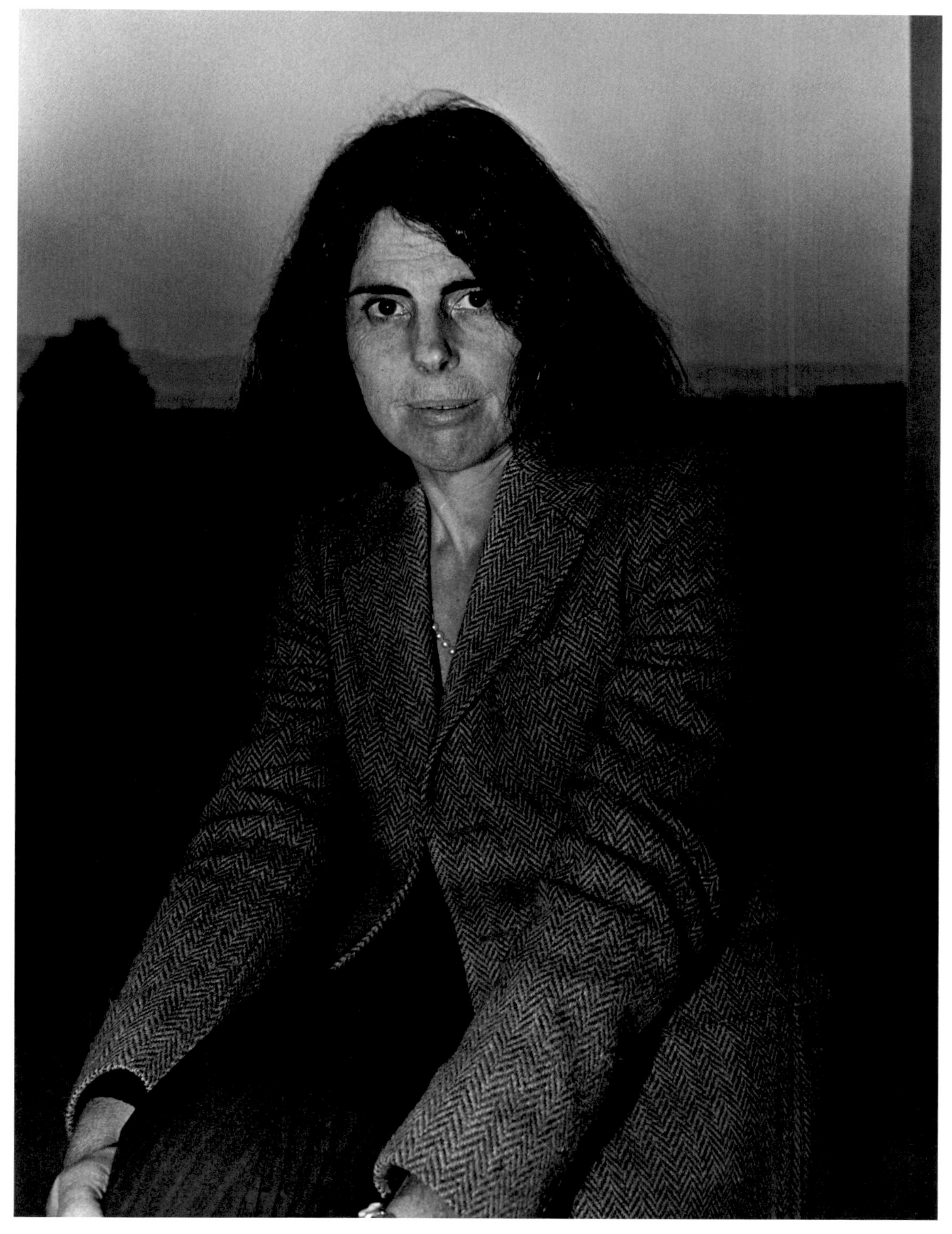

Margaret Walsh, Writer   1982

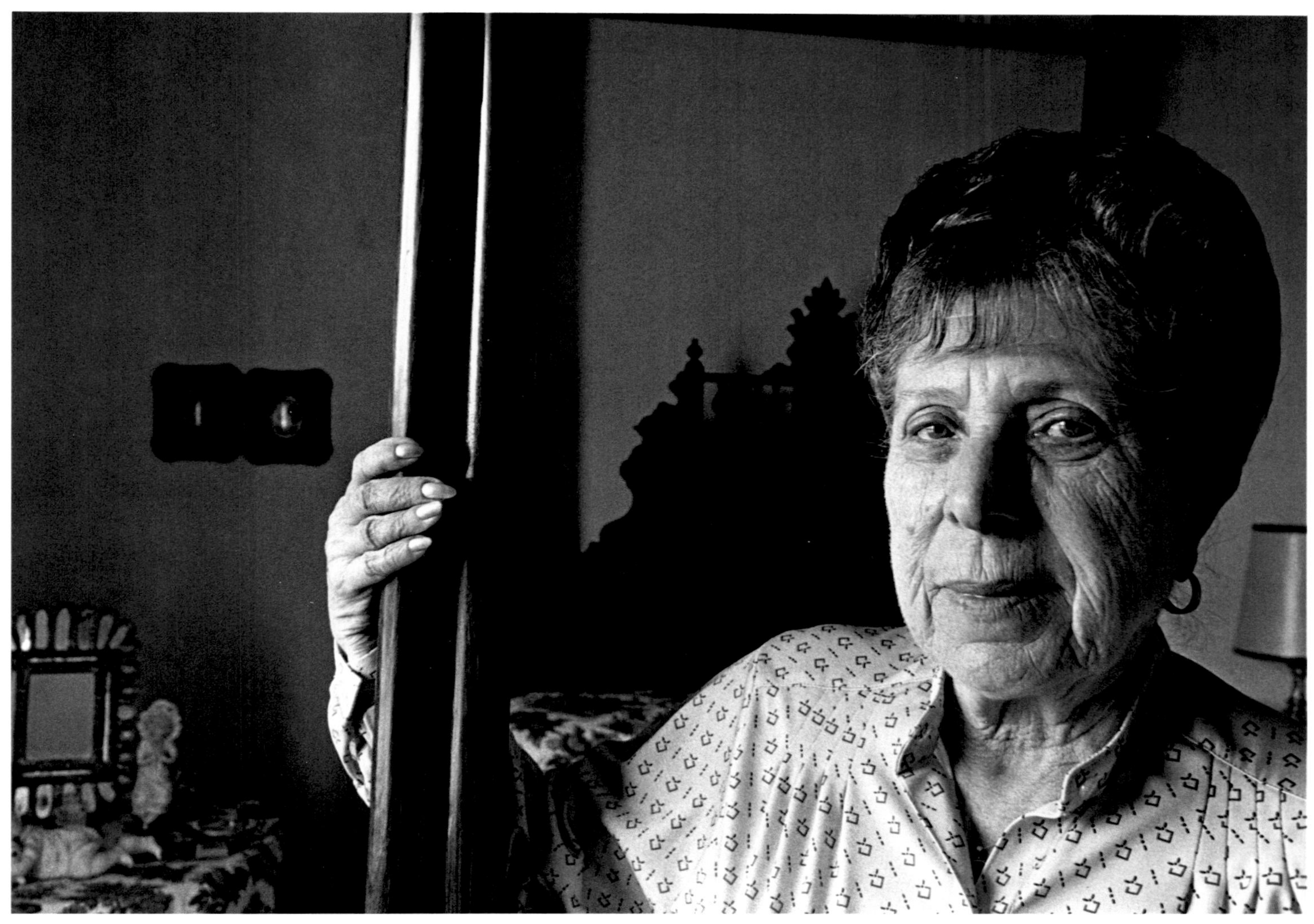

Pauline Aleaz, El Paso Doyenne   1982

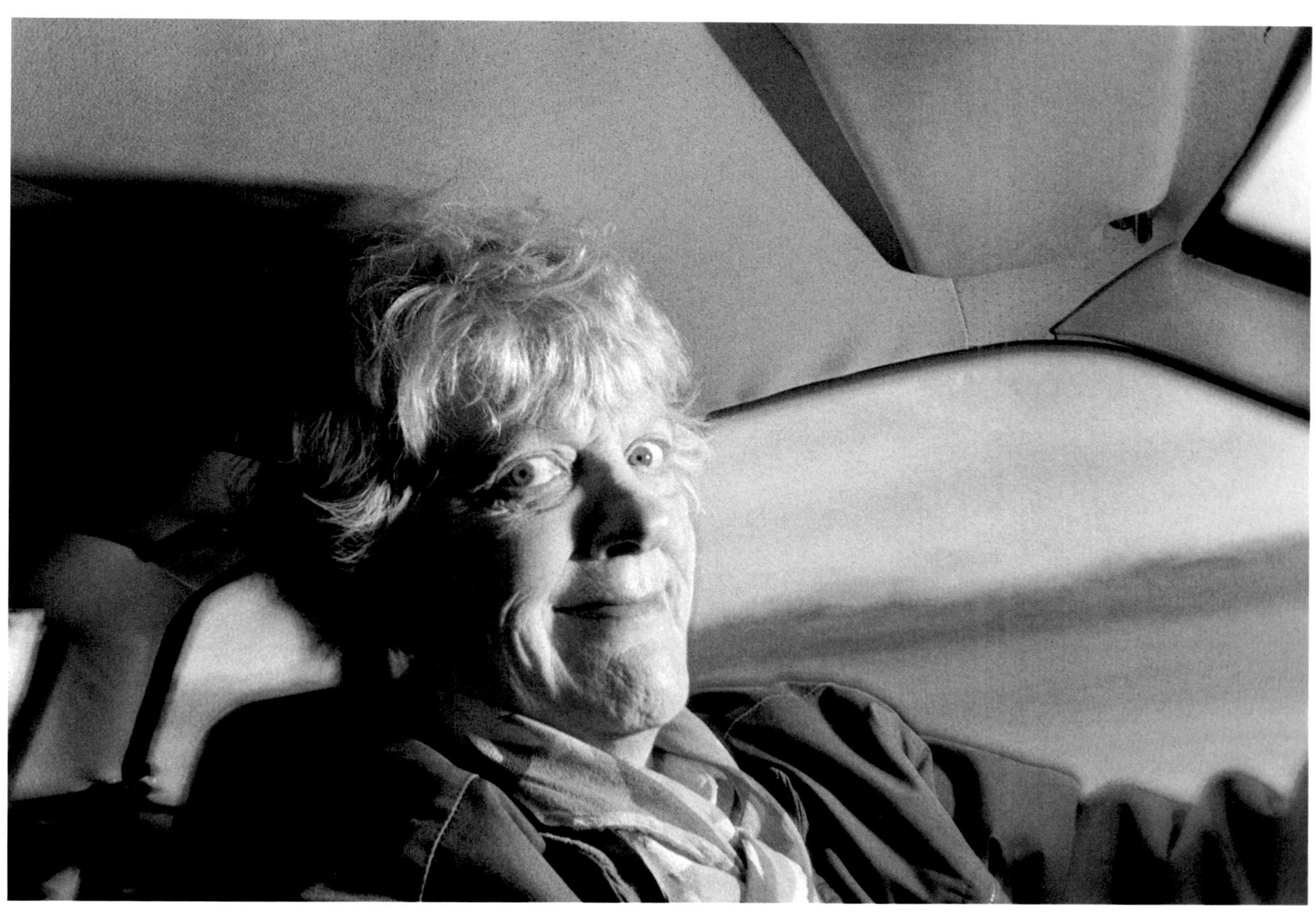

Myself as a Guggenheim Fellow   1982

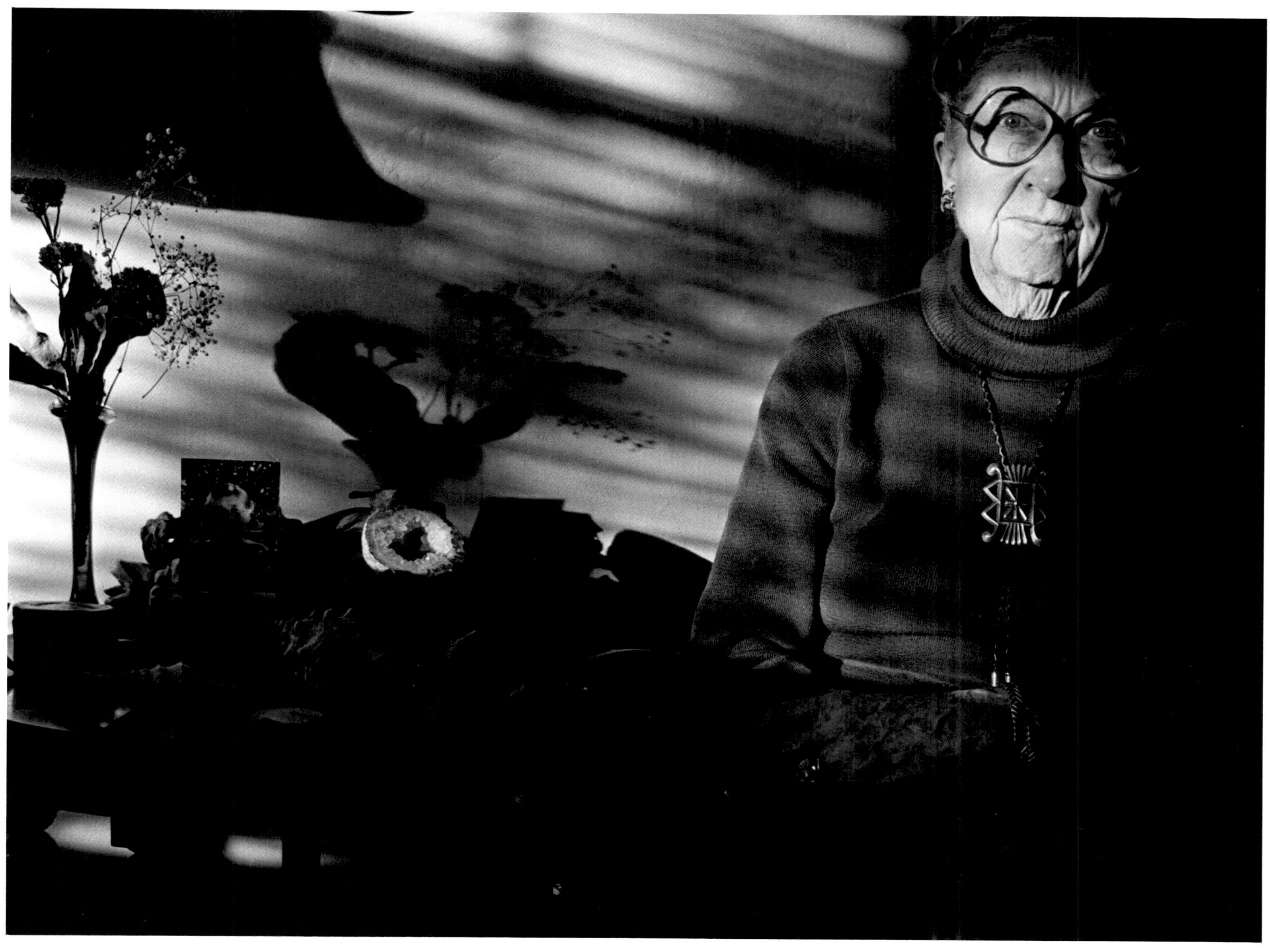

Helen Hobart   1982

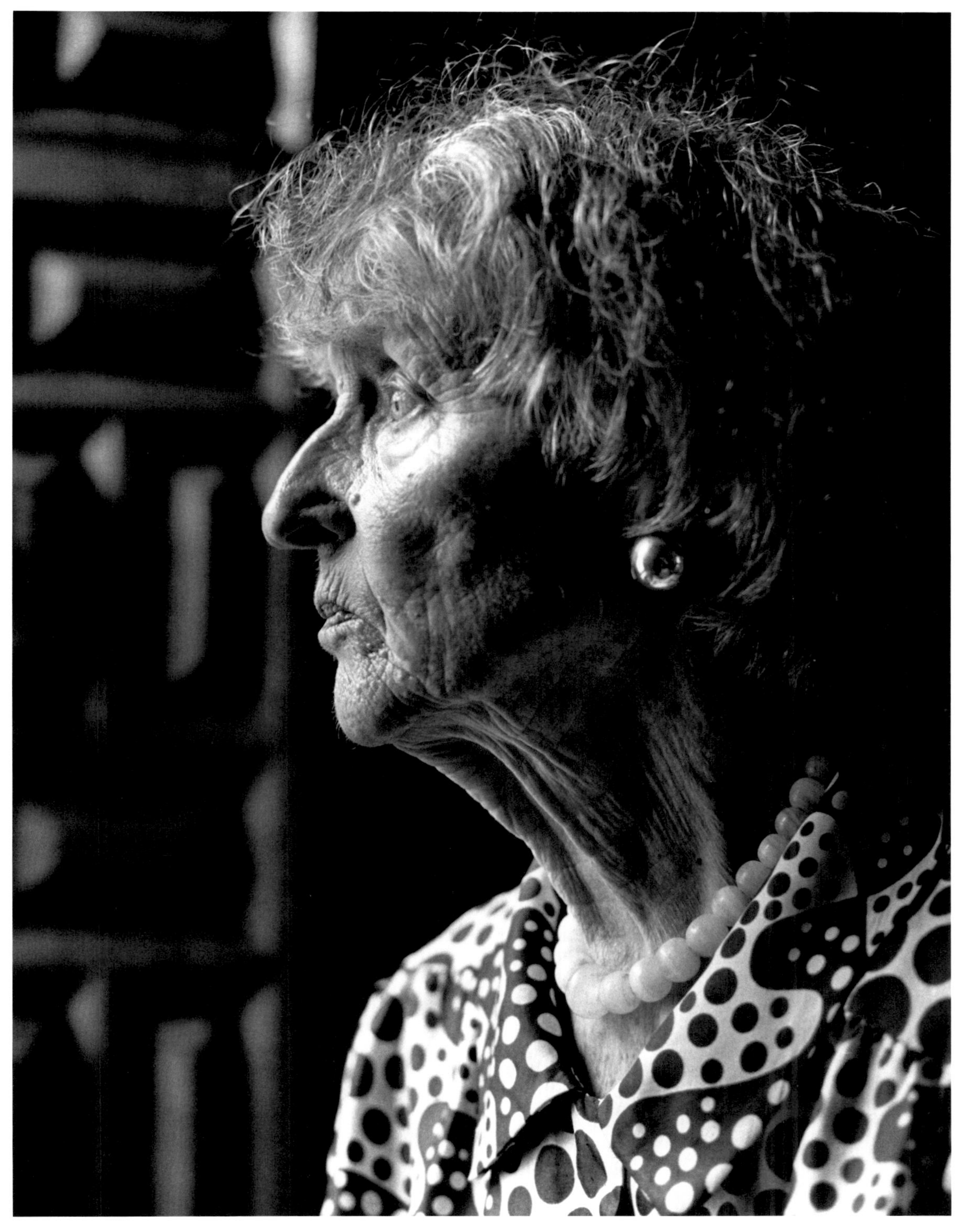

Profile of Yolanda   1982

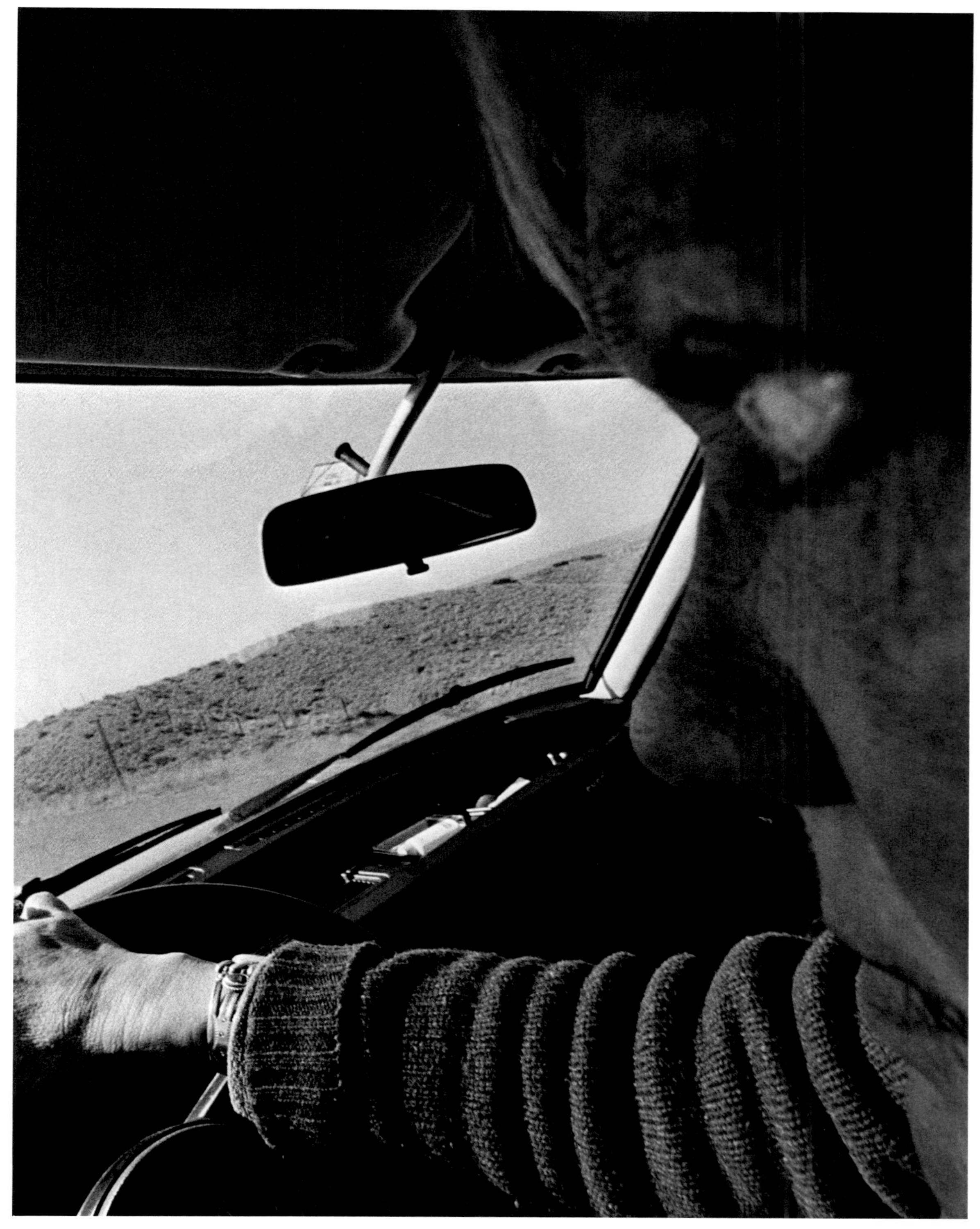

Southwest Passage   1982

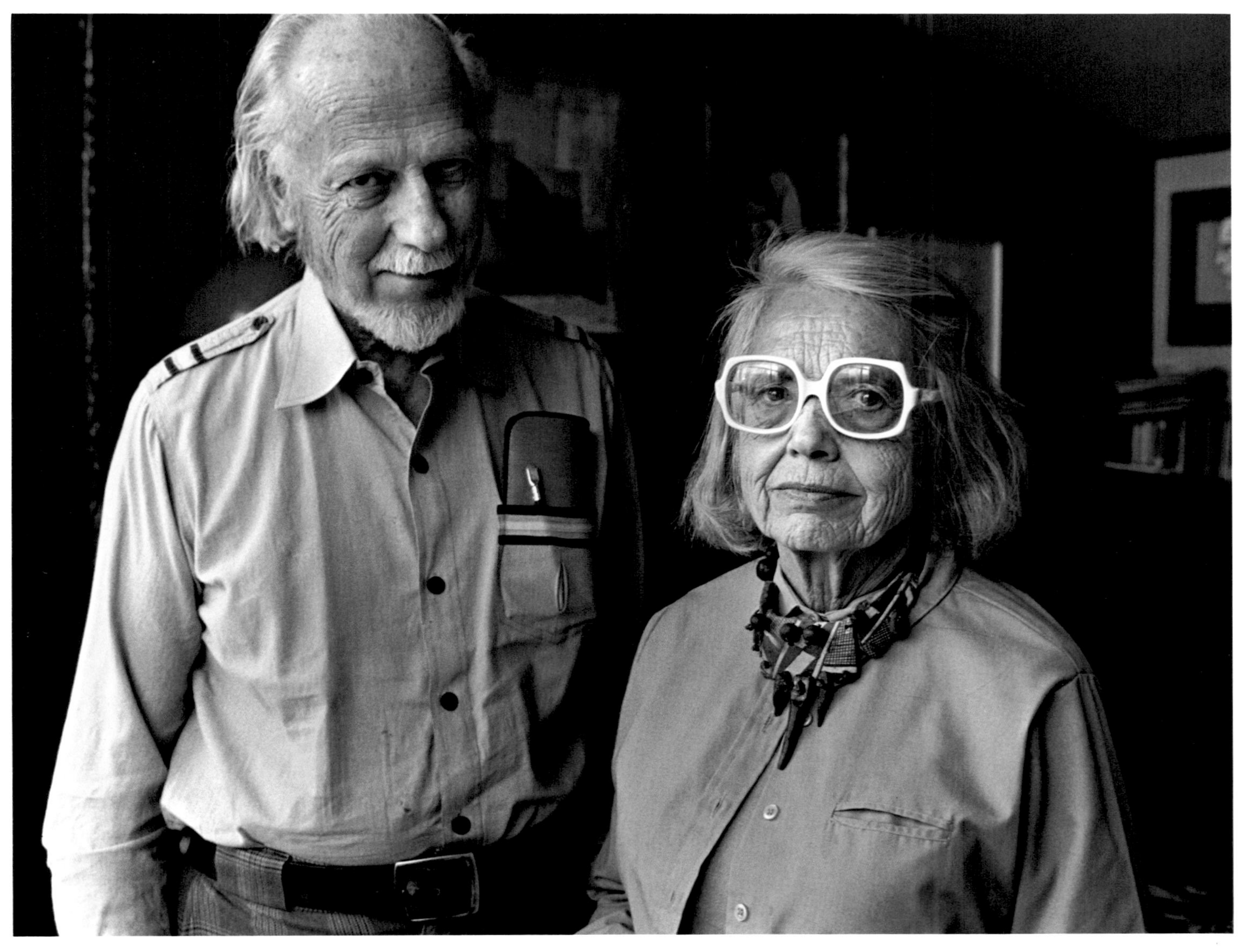

Charles Mattox, Sculptor, and His Wife, Dorothy   1982

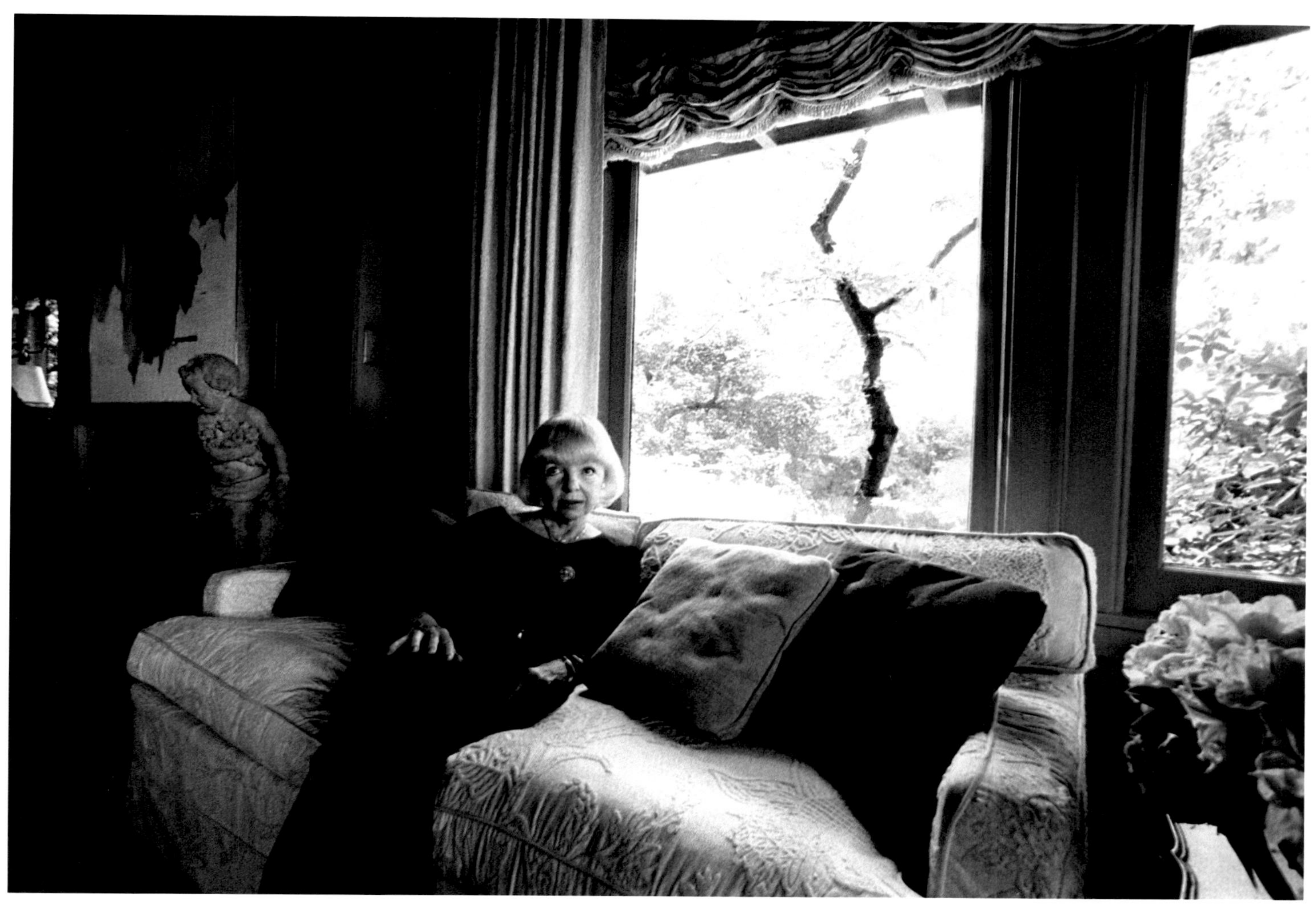
K. S., from a series *Seattle Faces*   1982

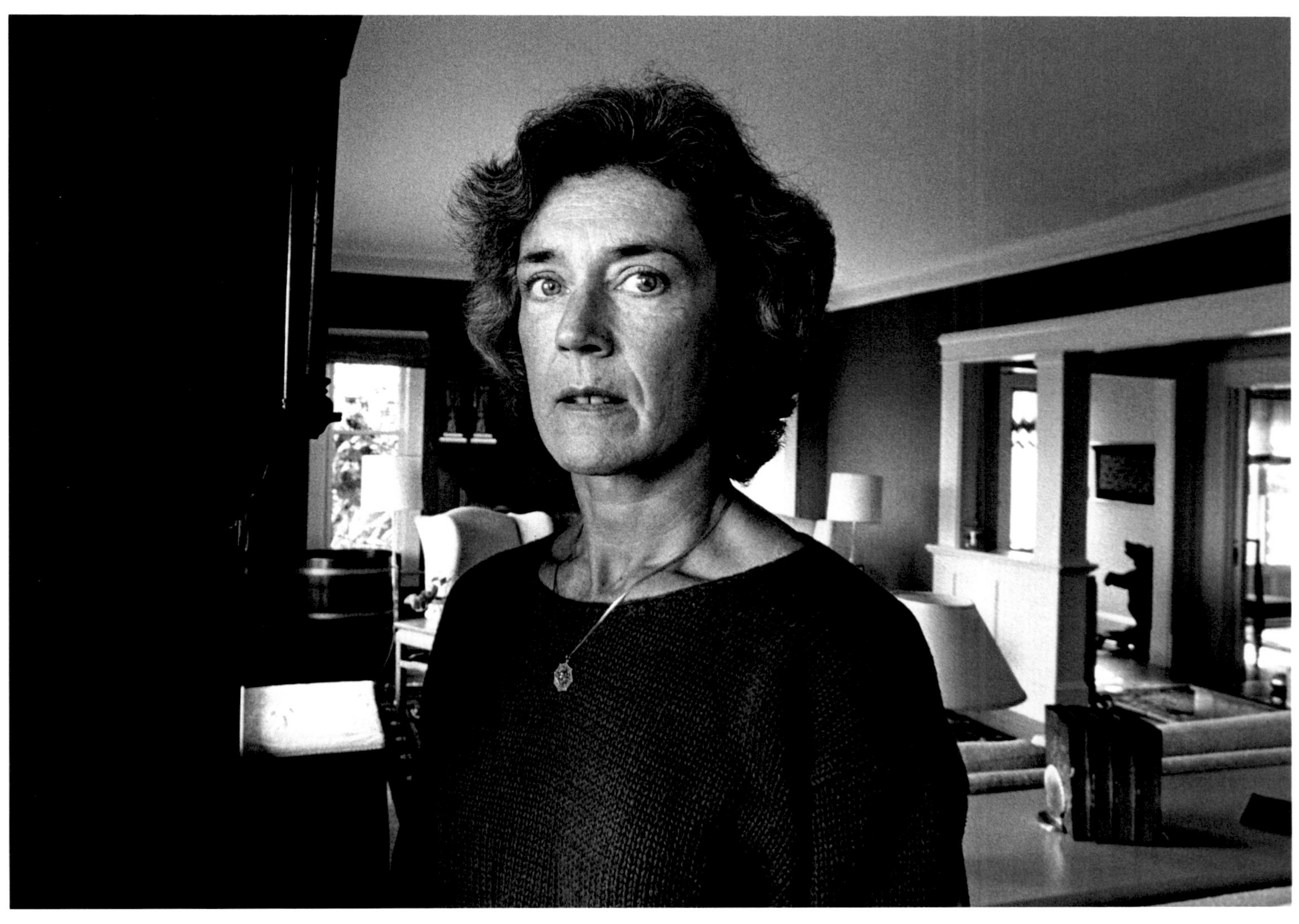 A. O., from a series *Seattle Faces*   1982

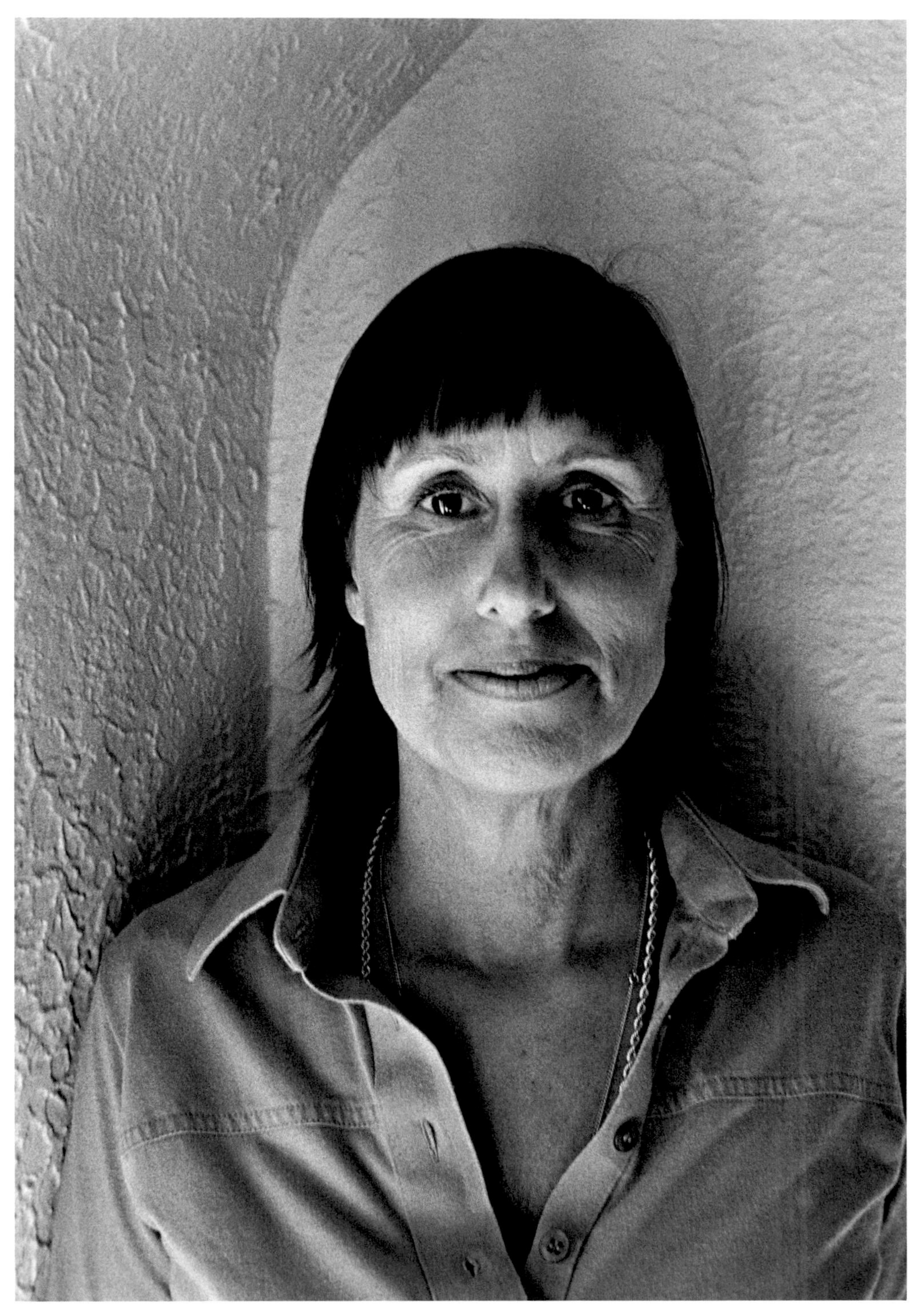

J. T., from a series *Seattle Faces*   1982

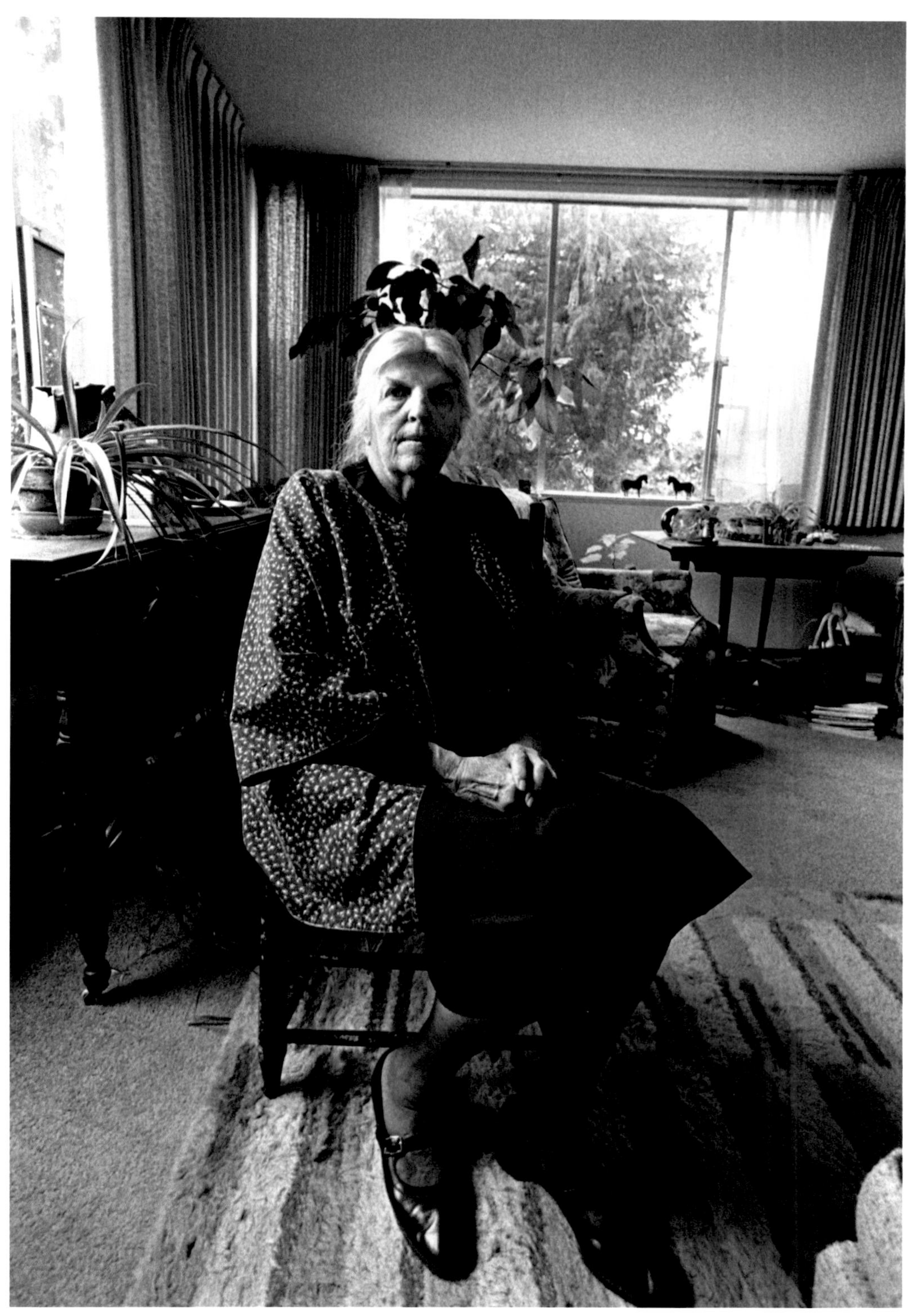

L. H., from a series *Seattle Faces*   1982

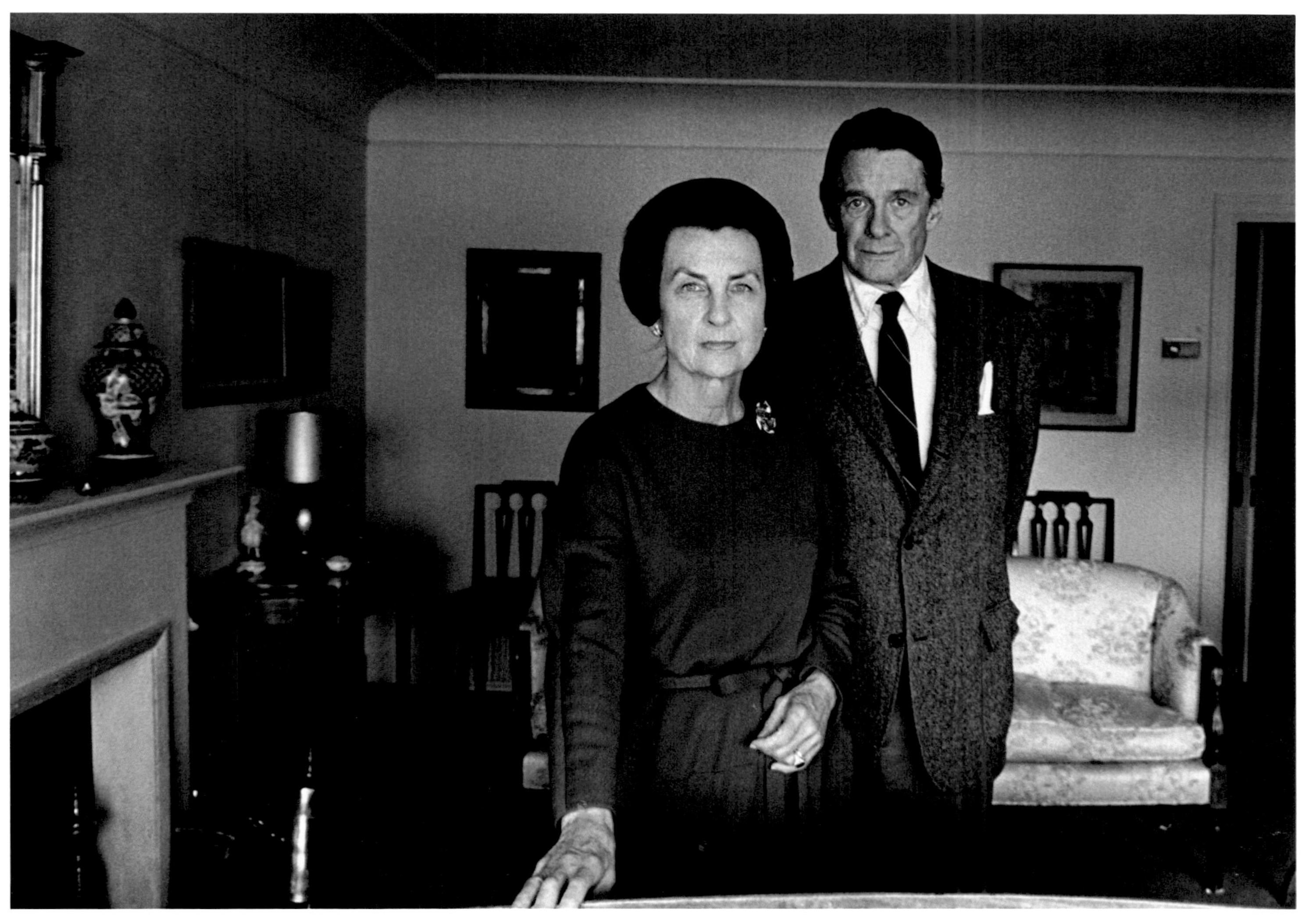

A. R. and D. R., from a series *Seattle Faces*   1982

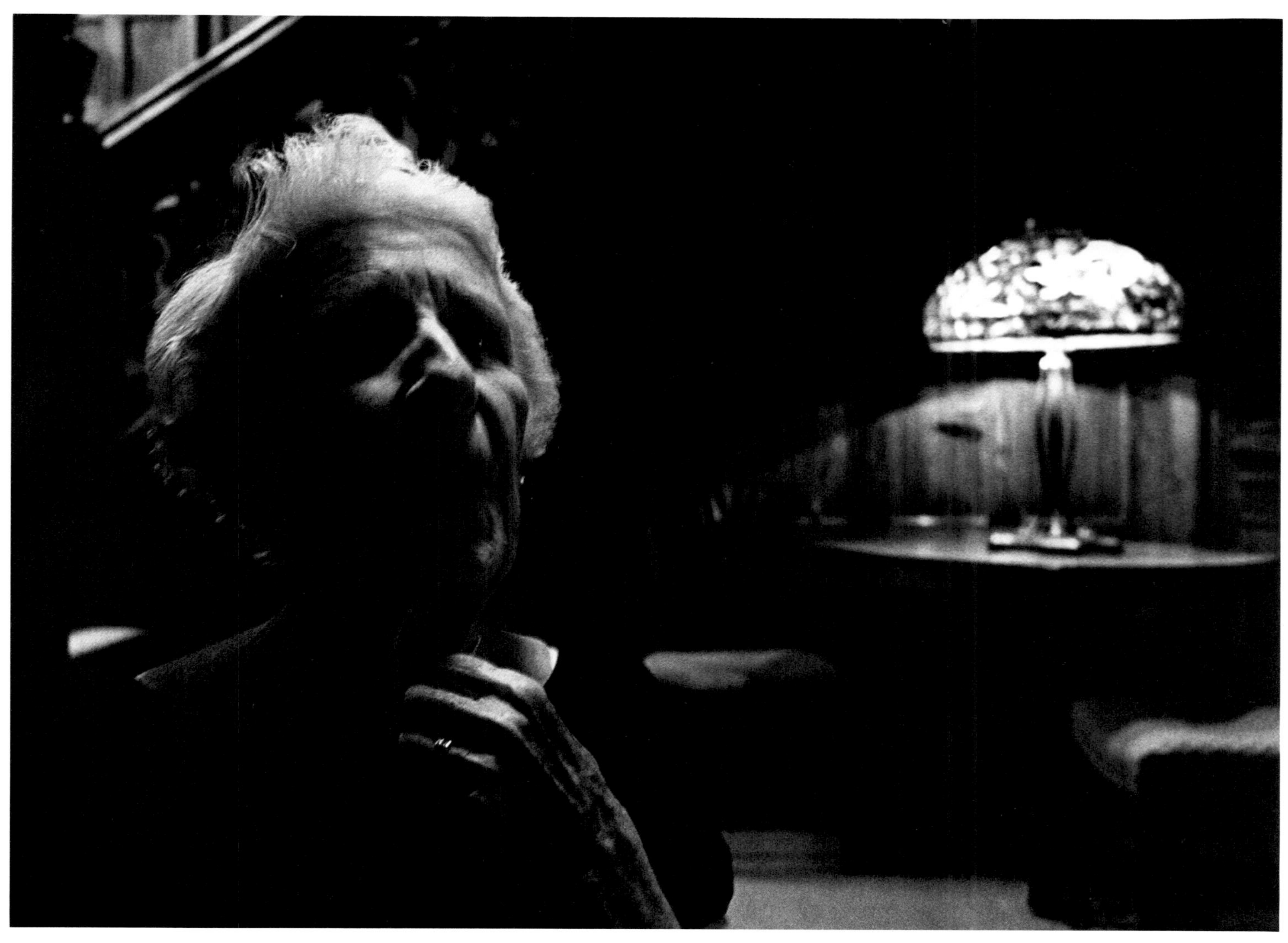

K. B., from a series *Seattle Faces*   1982

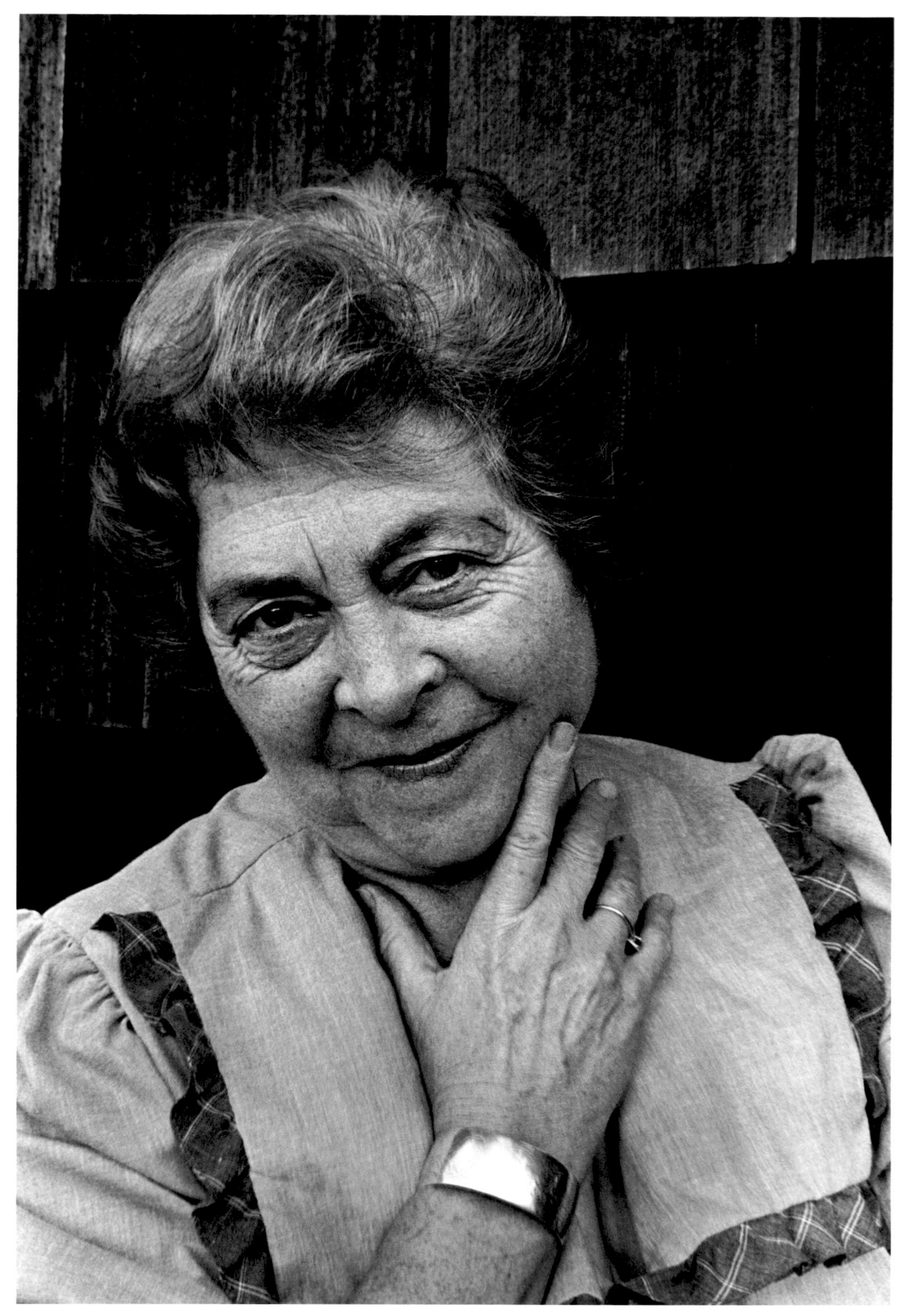

R. S., from a series *Seattle Faces*   1982

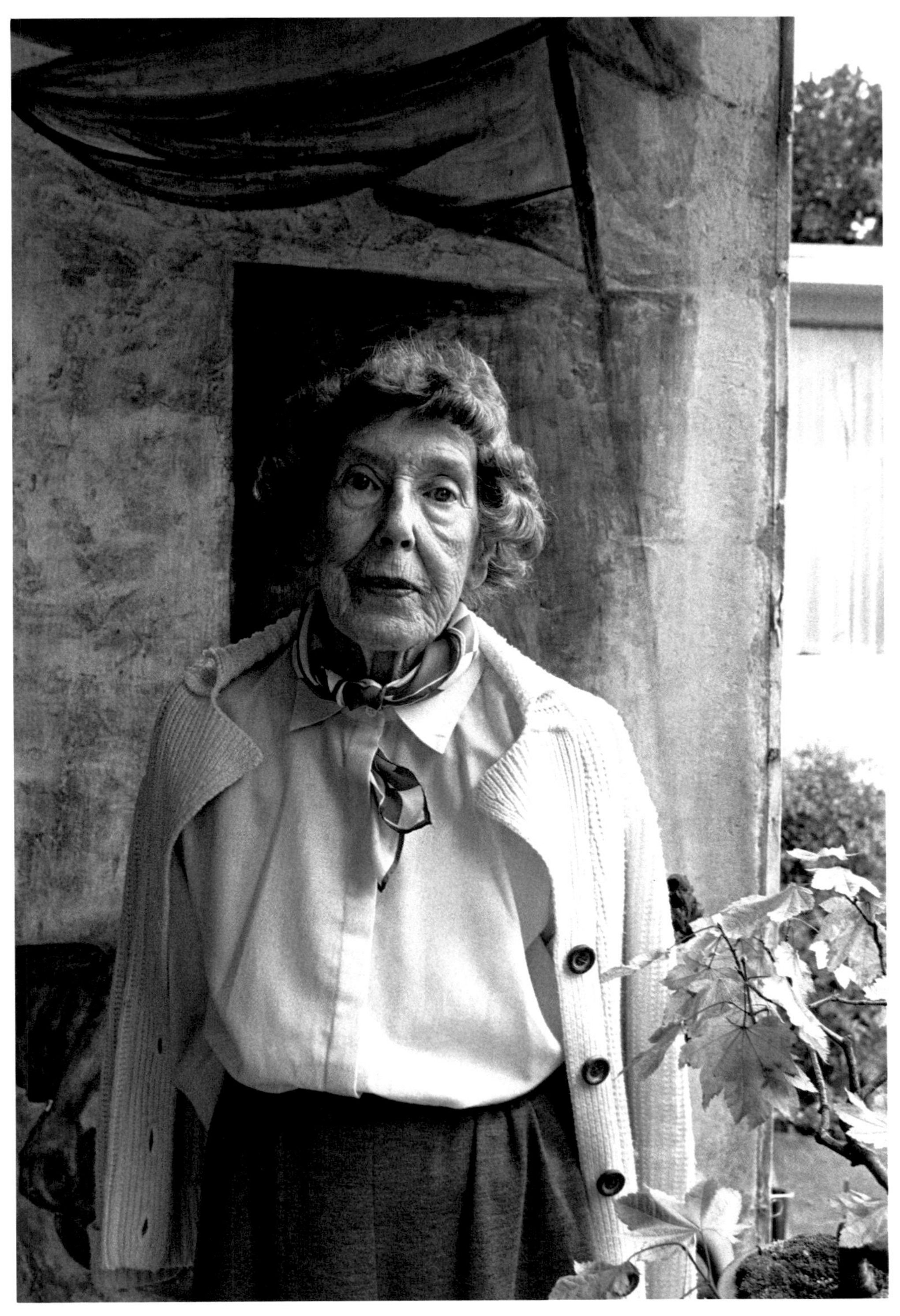

V. P., from a series *Seattle Faces*   1982

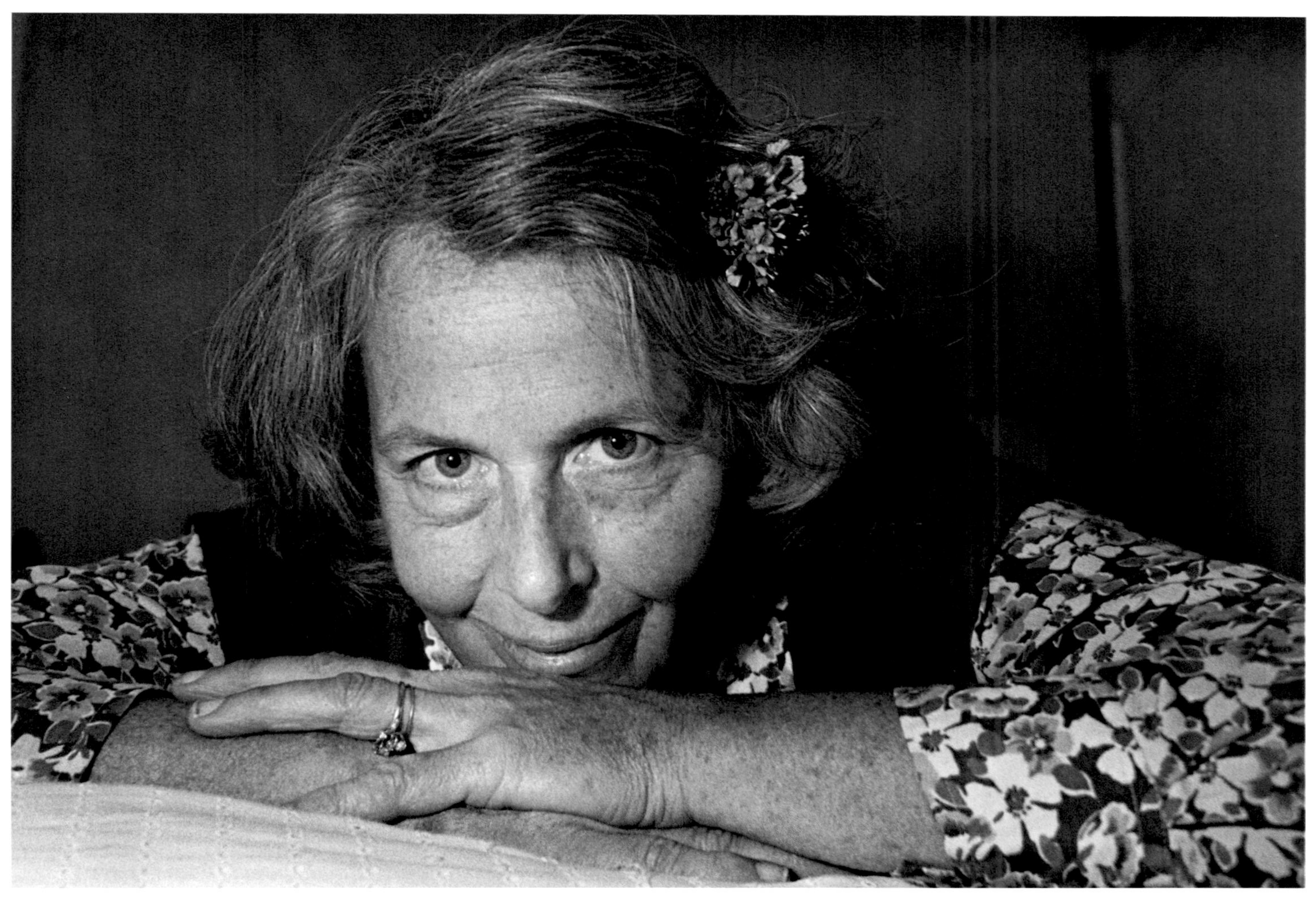

N. B., from a series *Seattle Faces*   1982

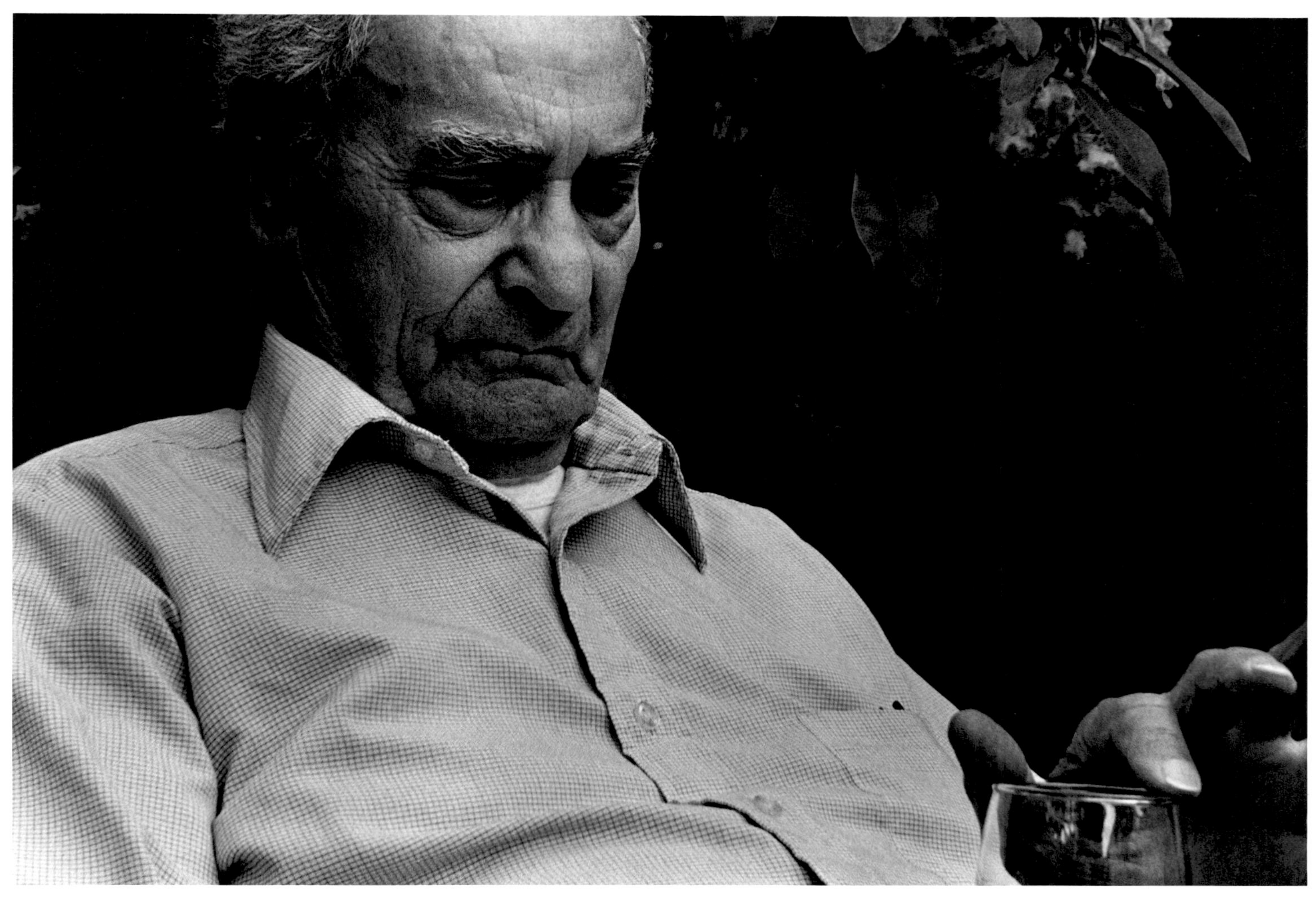

A. P., from a series *Seattle Faces*   1982

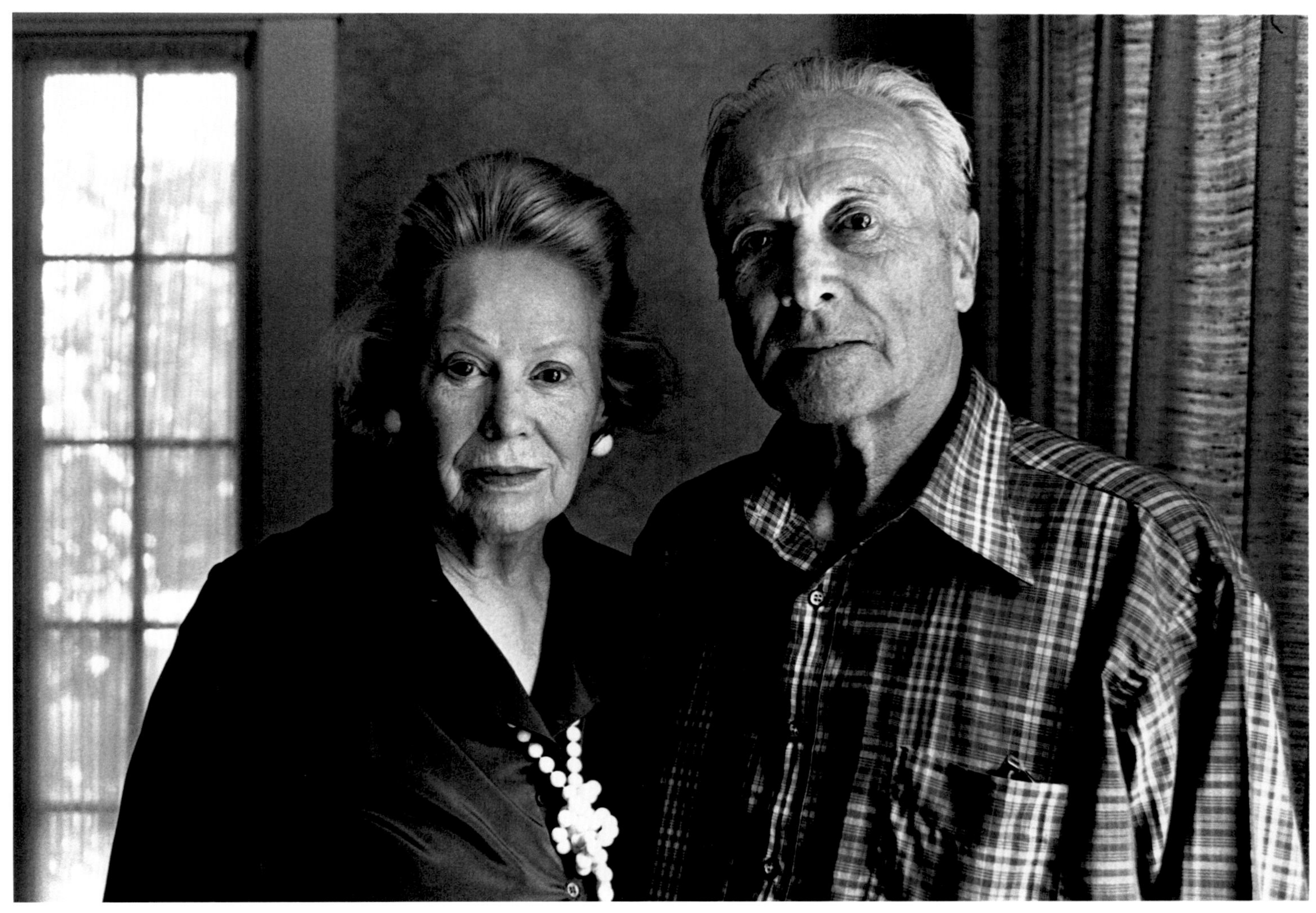

B. A. and W. A., from a series *Seattle Faces*   1982

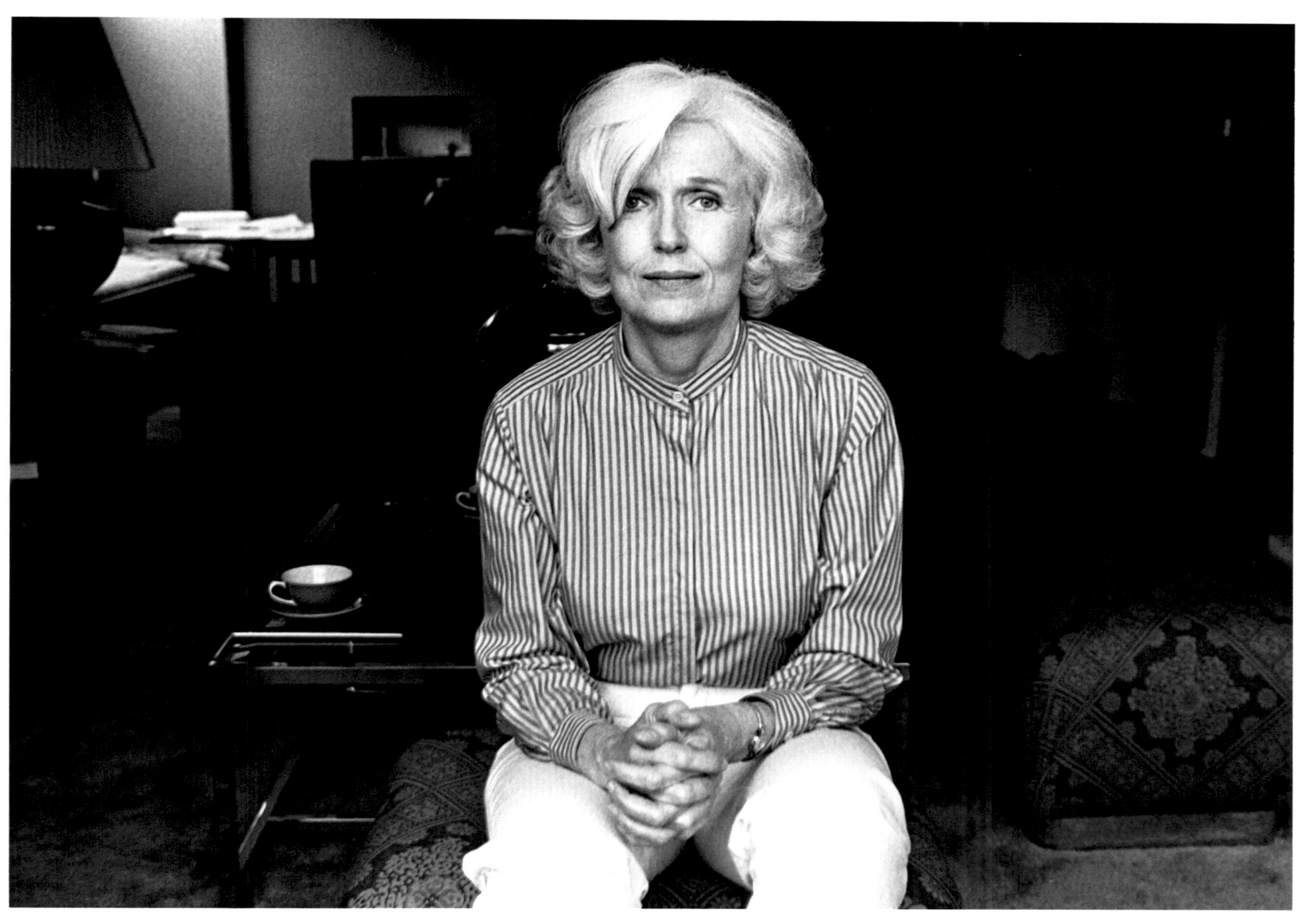

B. B., from a series *Seattle Faces*   1982

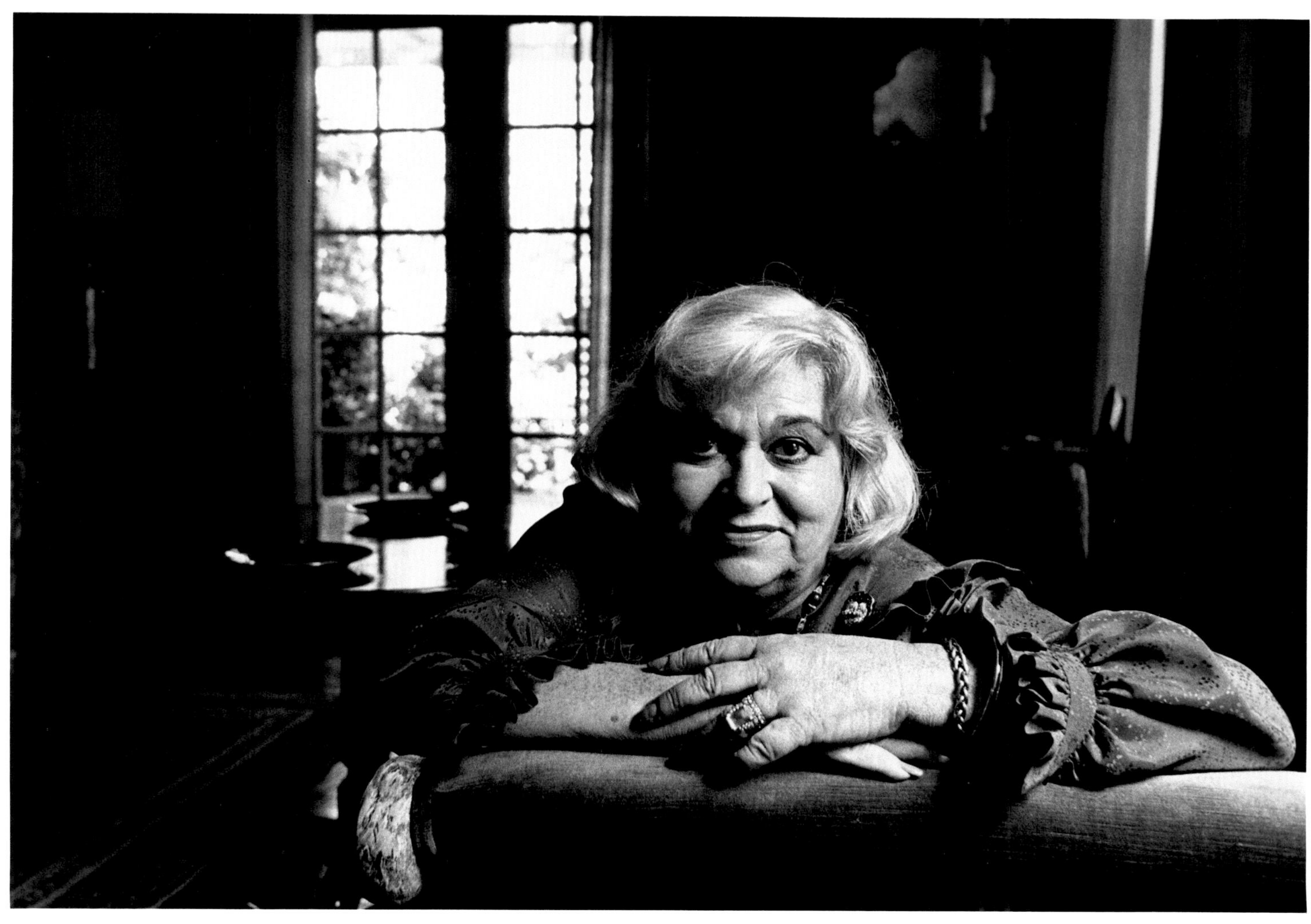

H. M. W., from a series *Seattle Faces*   1982

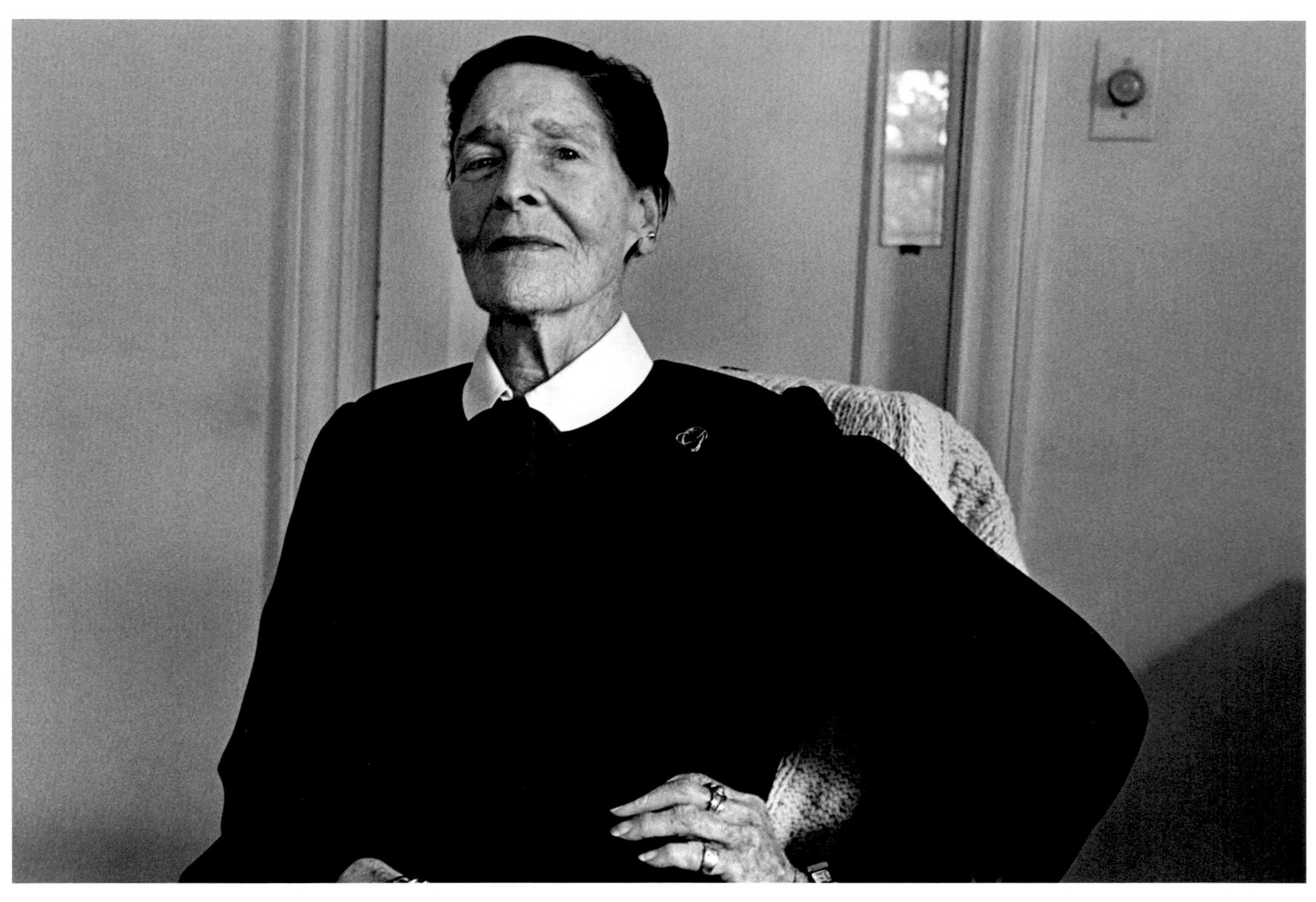

J. E., from a series *Seattle Faces*   1982

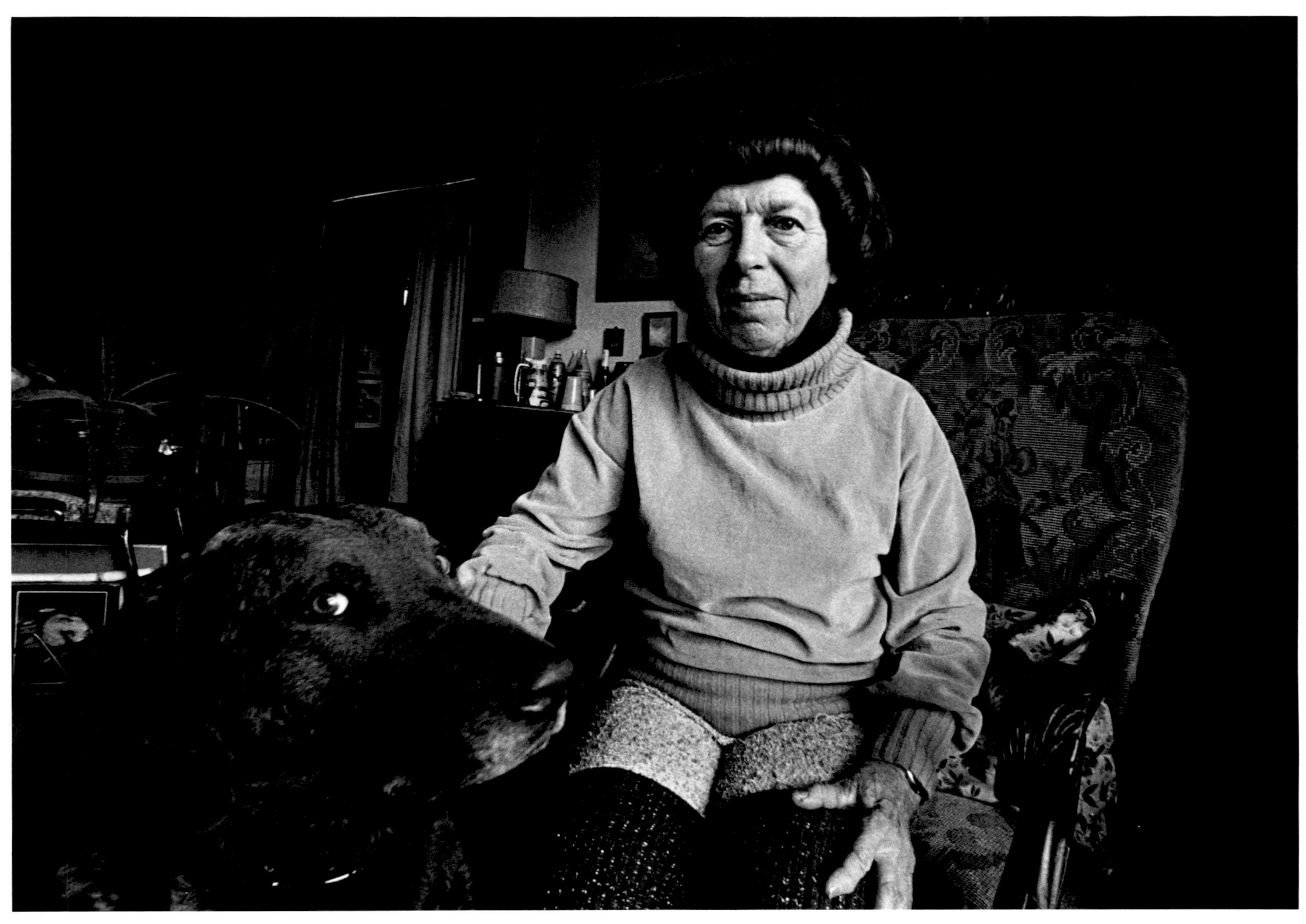

Winnie Beasley, Flyer   1983

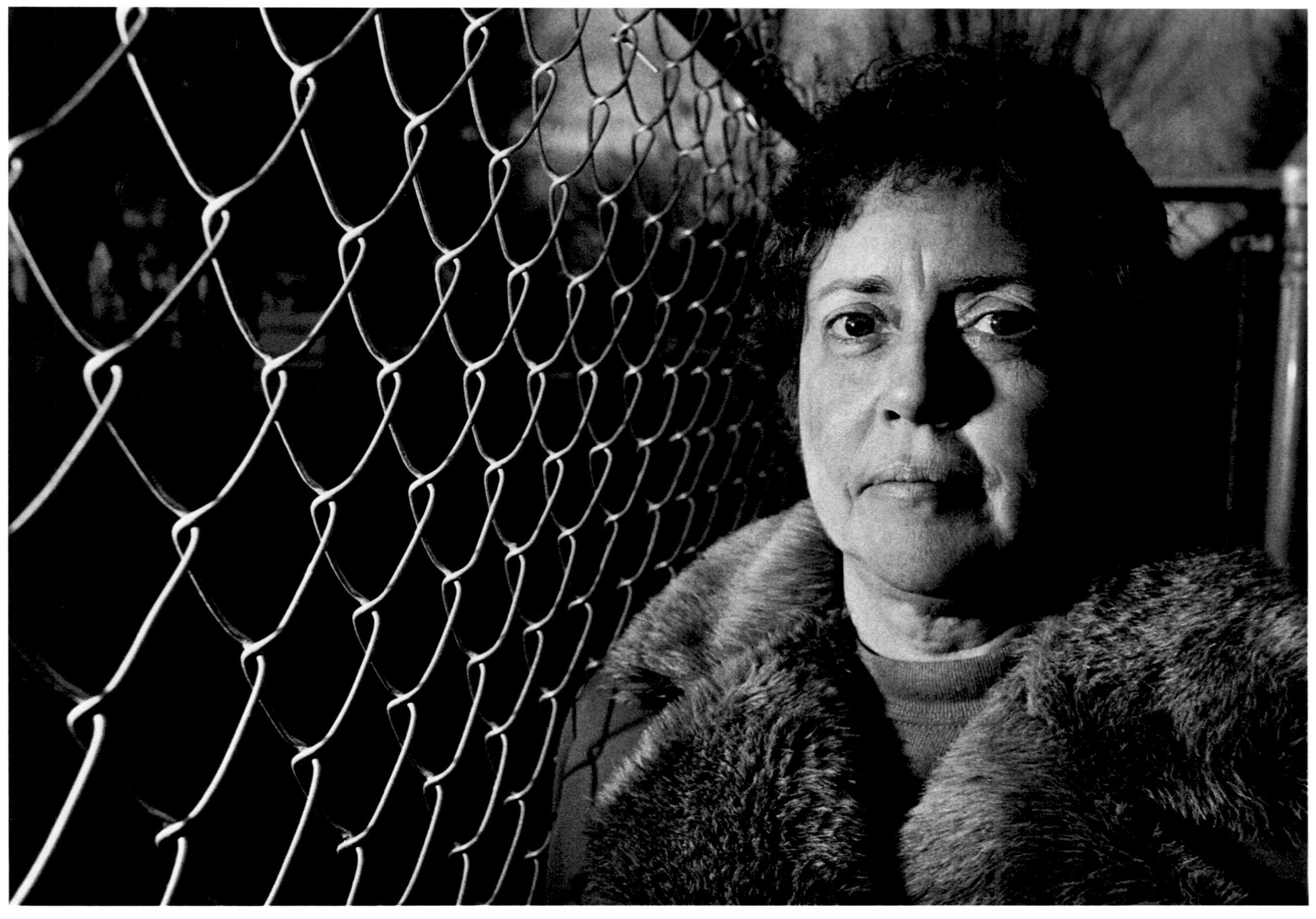

Donna Humble, Copywriter   1983

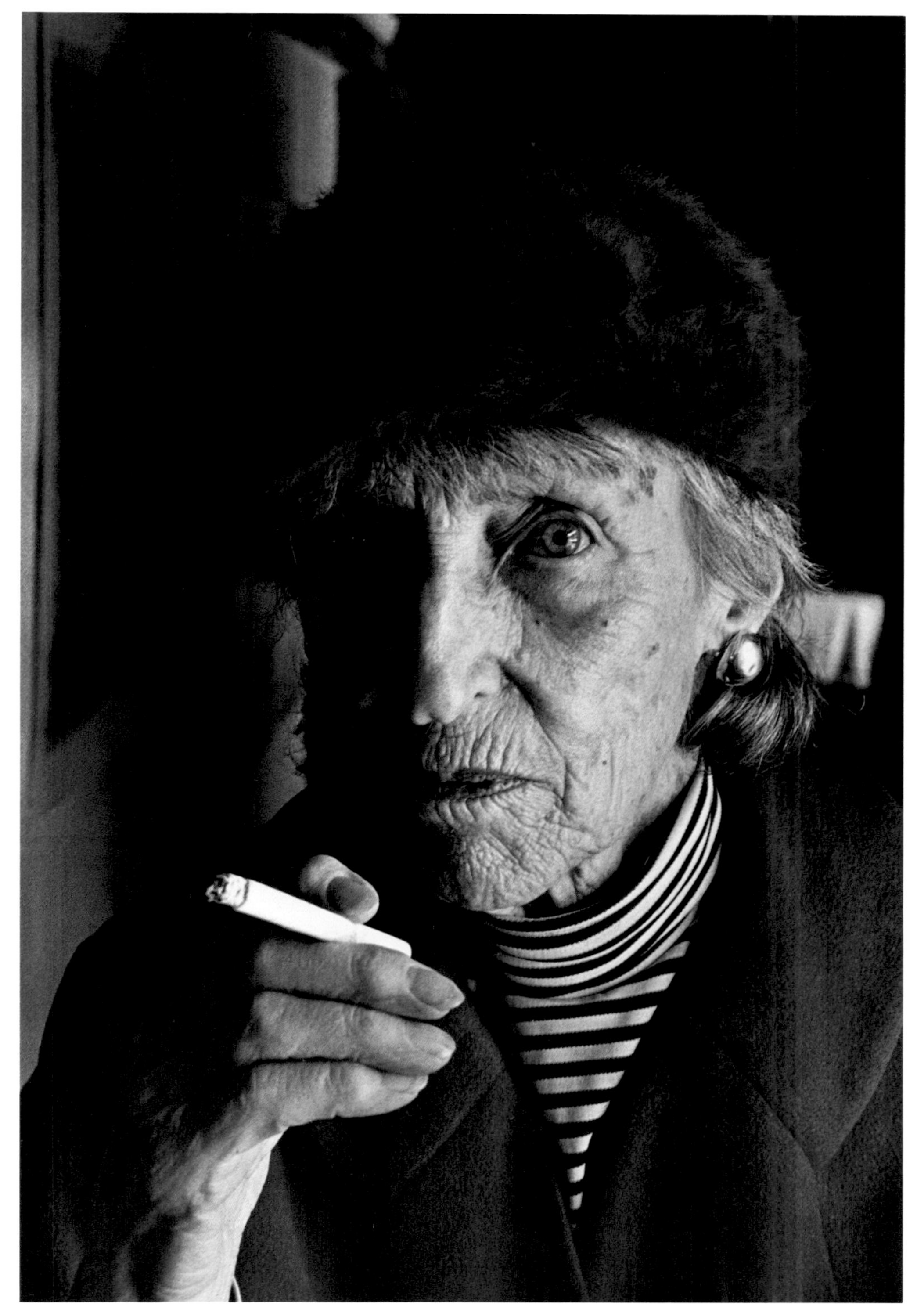

Yolanda   1983

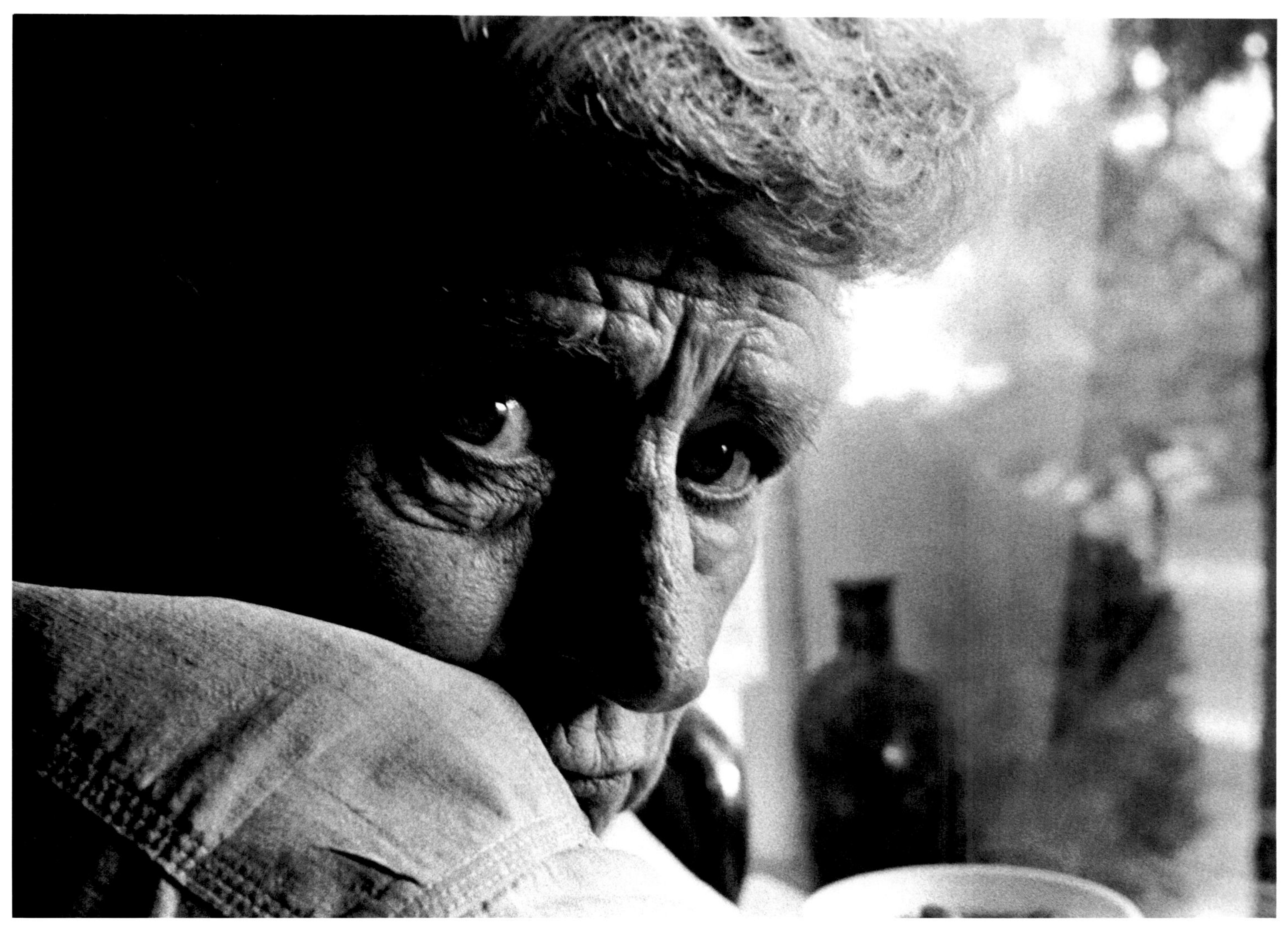

Shelley   1983

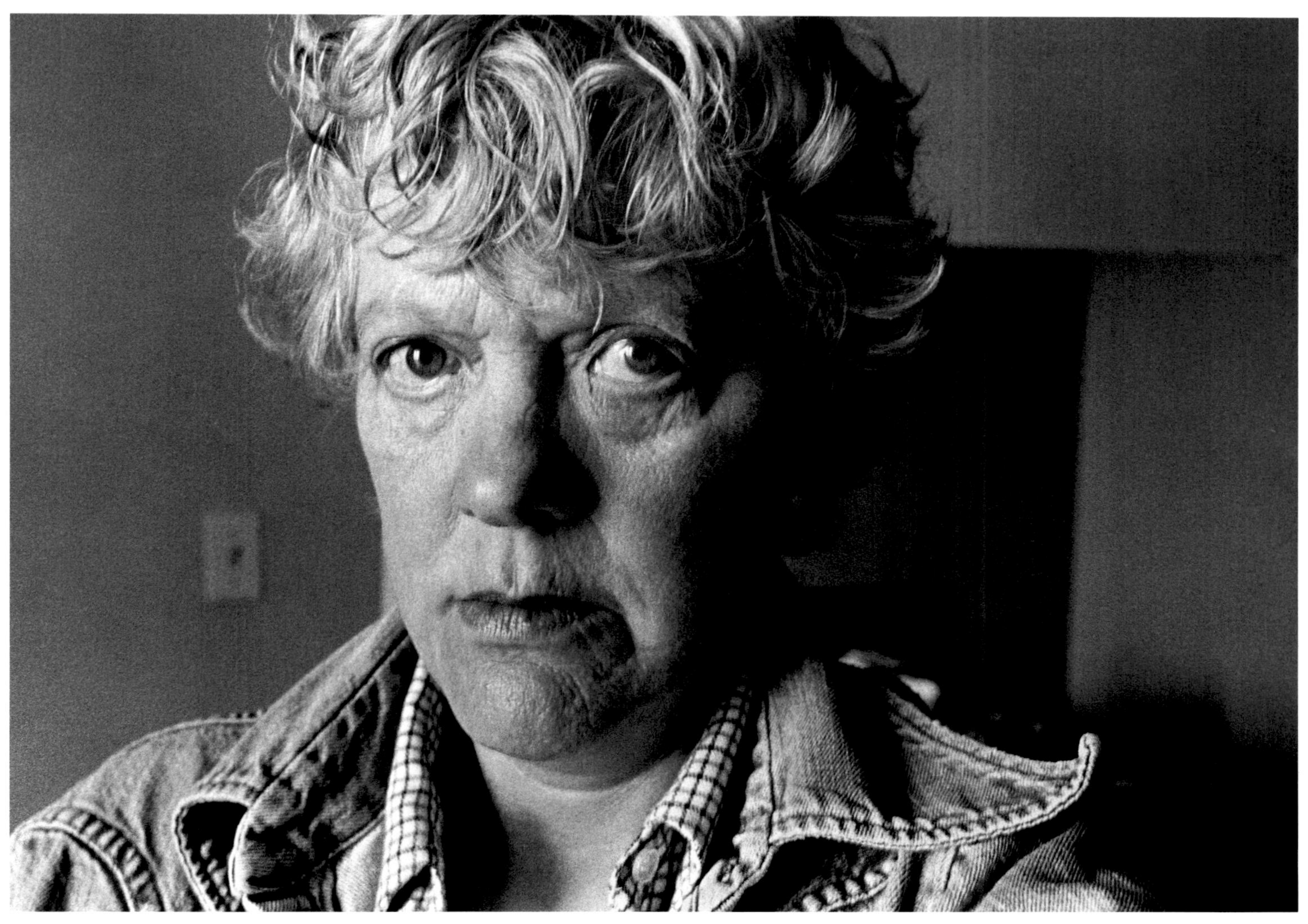

Myself in Amarillo   1983

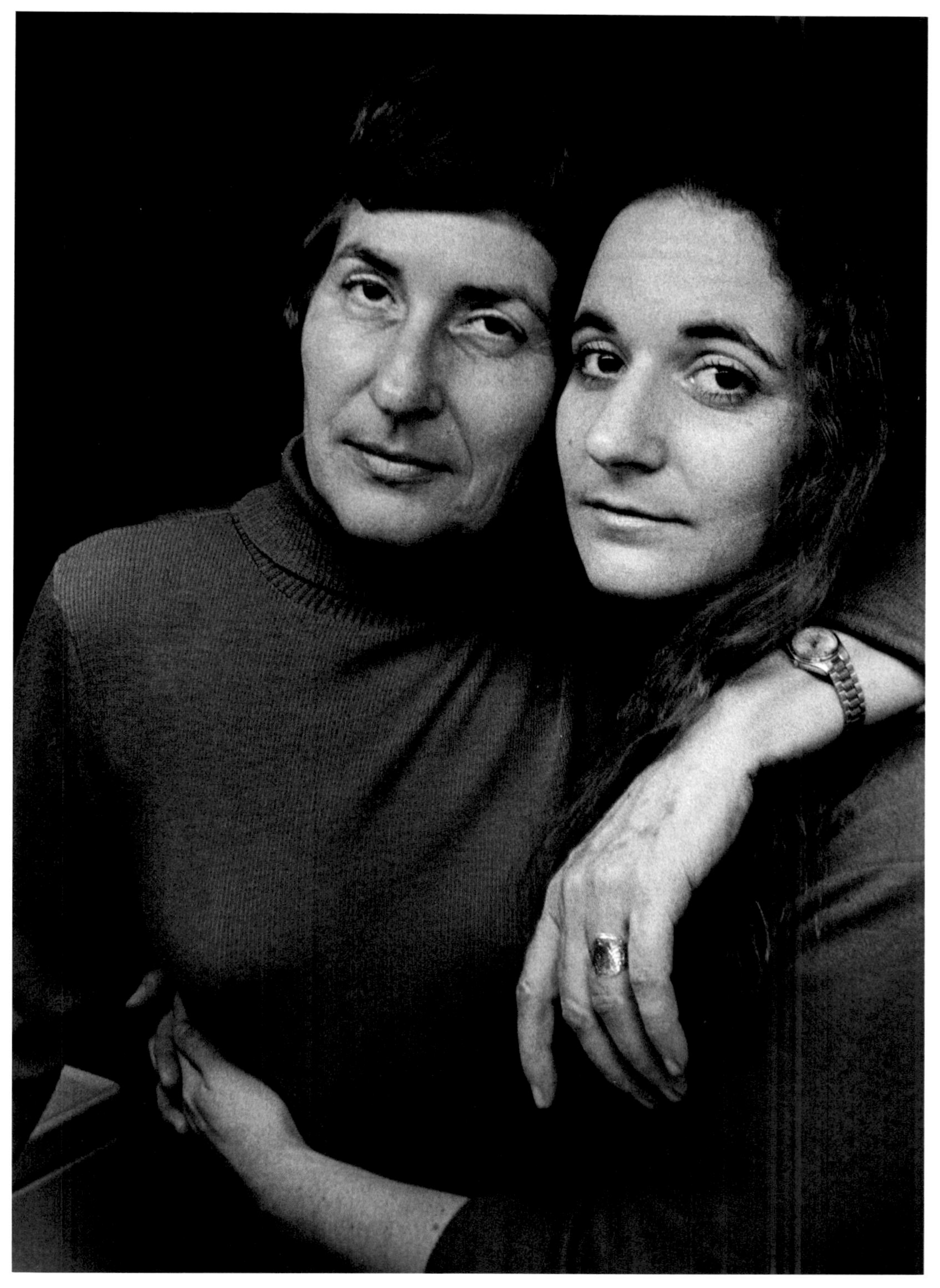

JoAnn Cockelreas and Her Daughter Jean, Commerce, Texas   1983

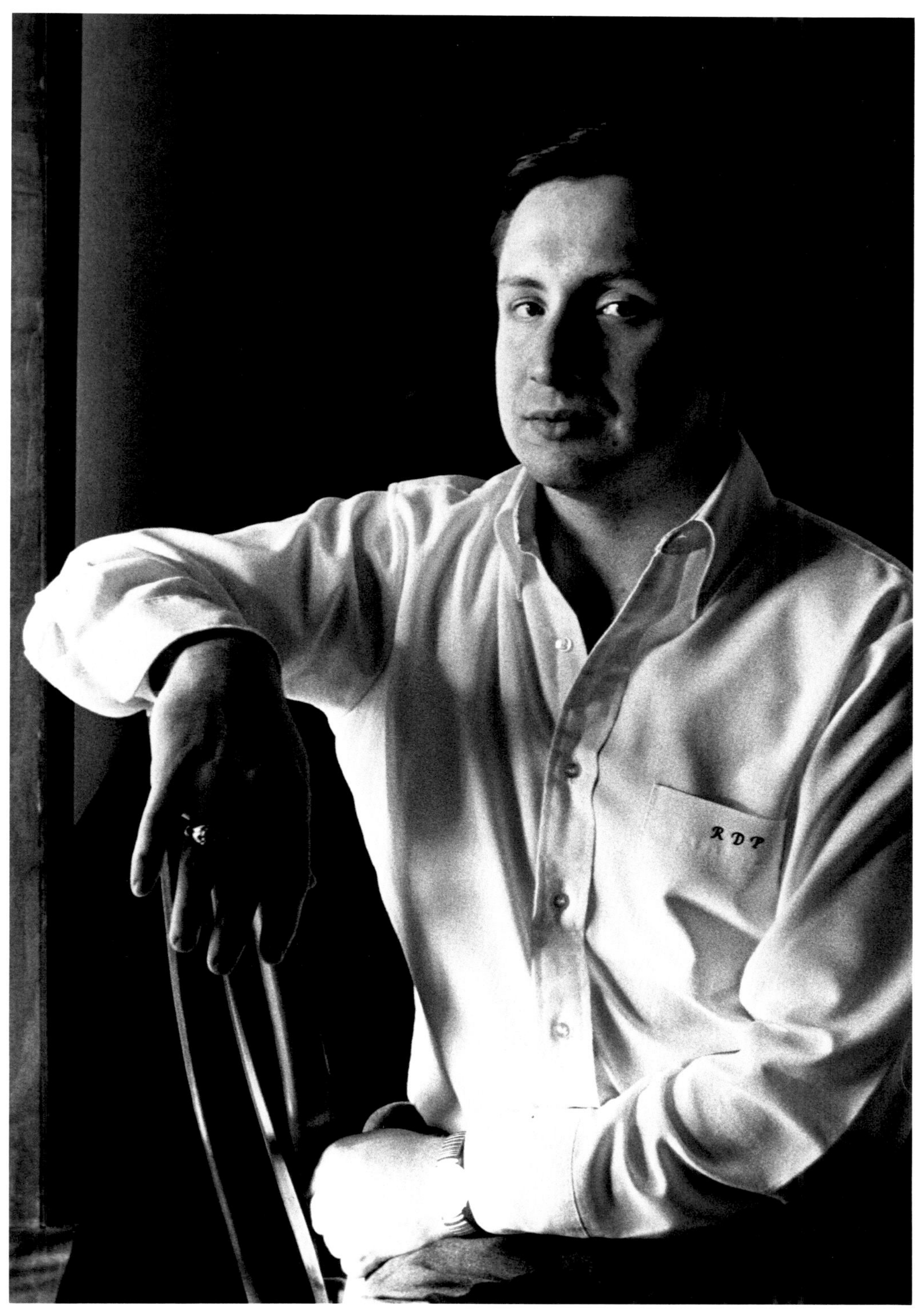

Richard Parrish, Commerce, Texas   1983

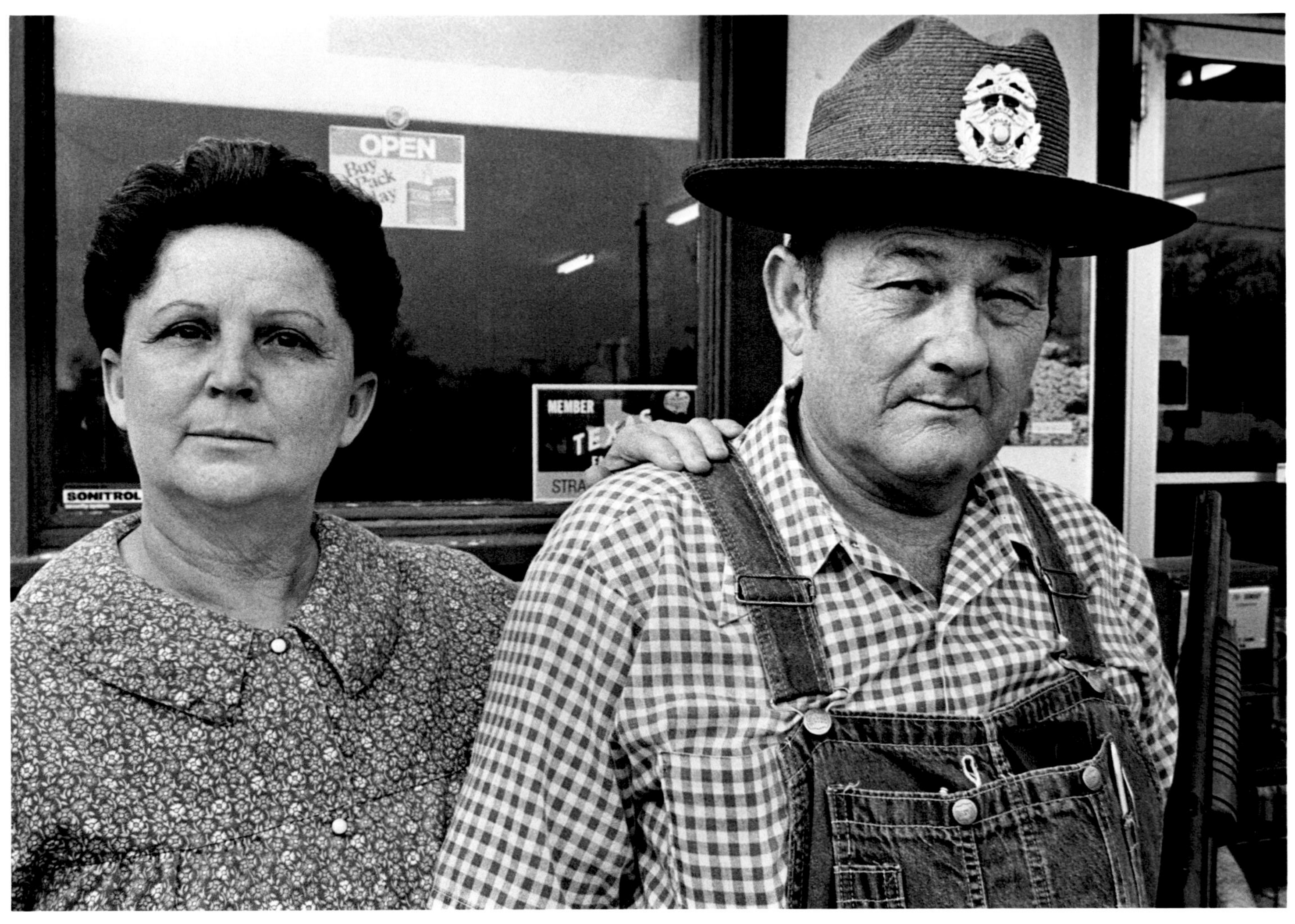

B. J. and Mary Jo Garner, Commerce, Texas, 1983

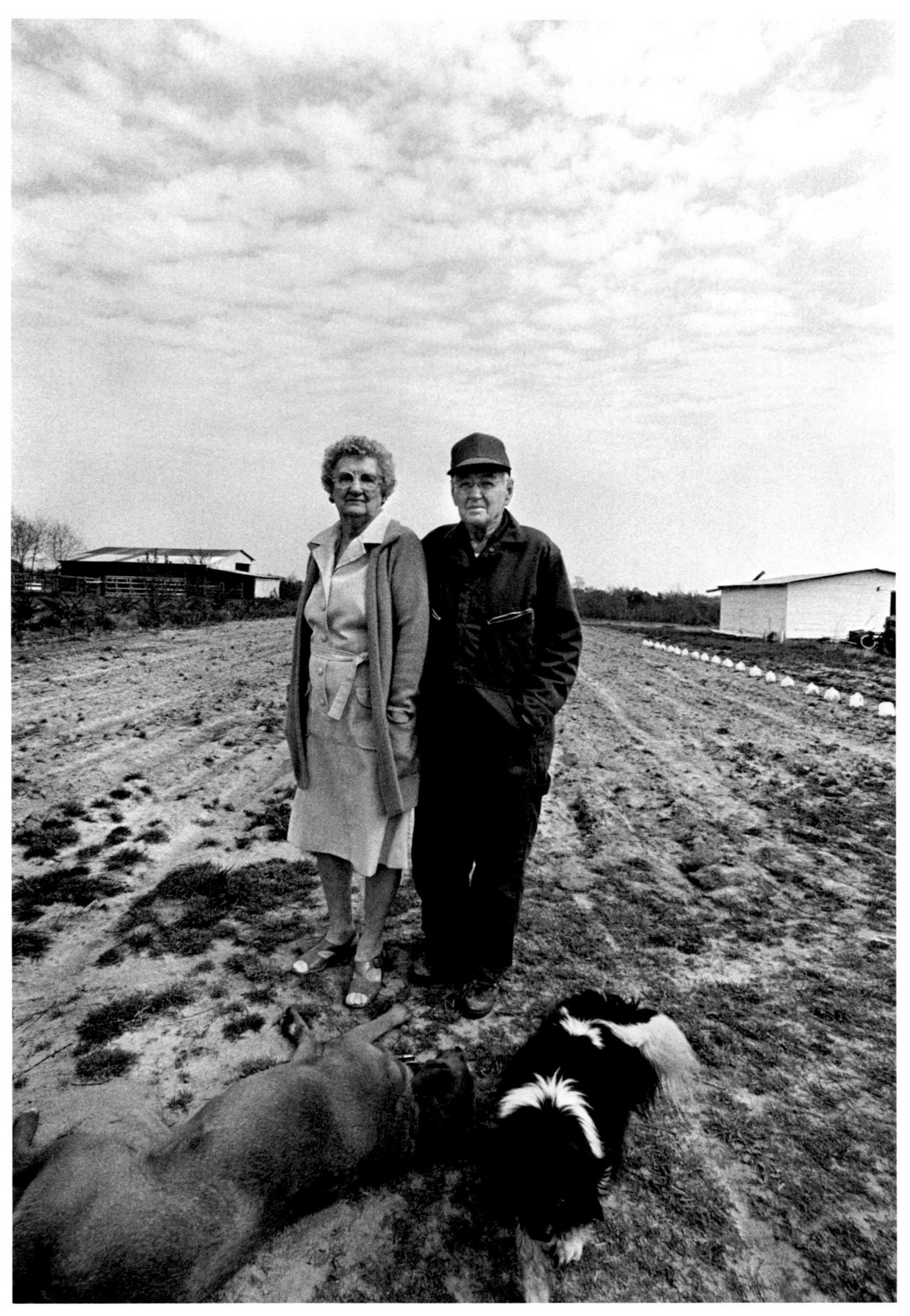

Chester and Kittie Gibbs, Commerce, Texas, 1983

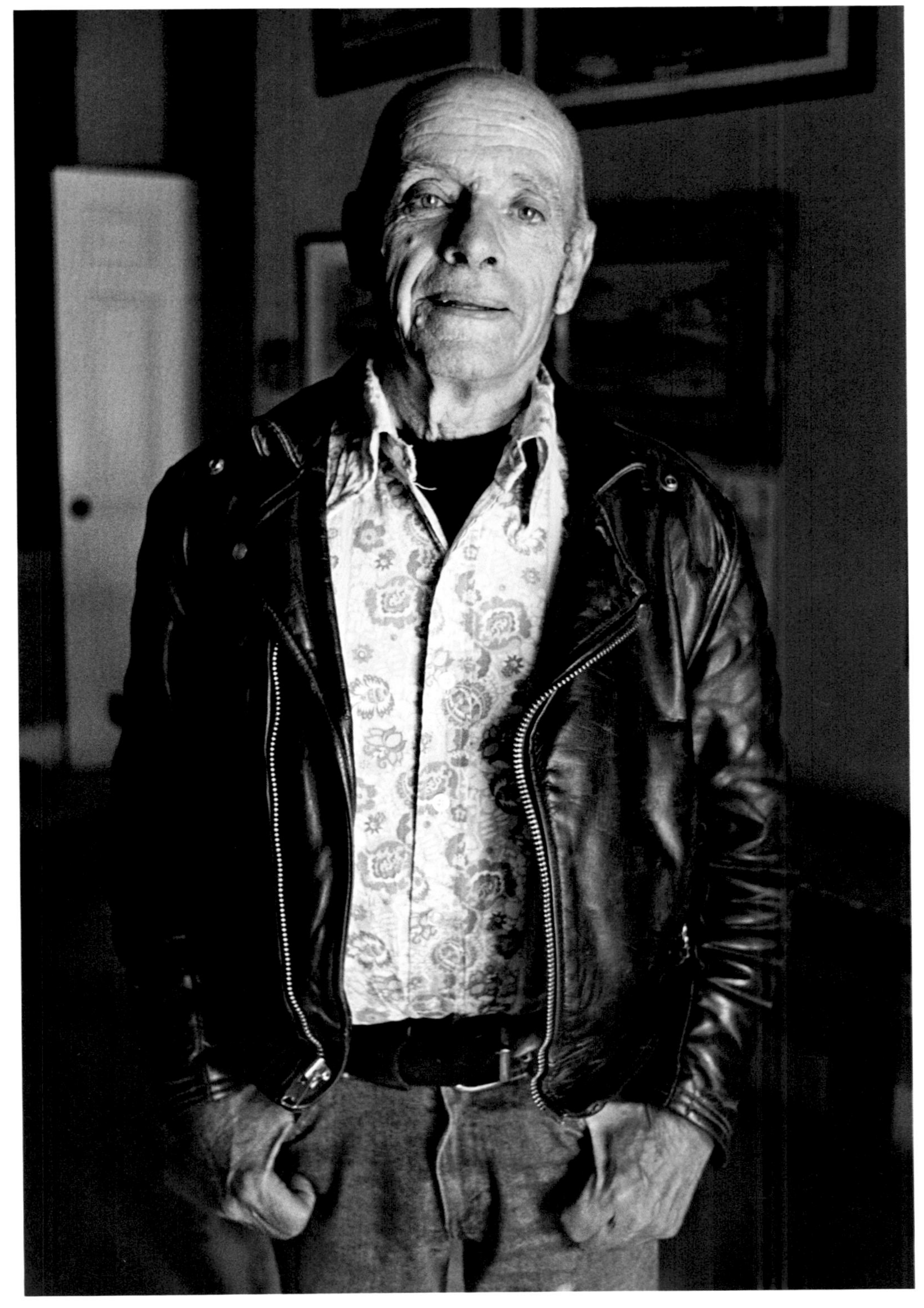

J. B. Jackson, author, 1983

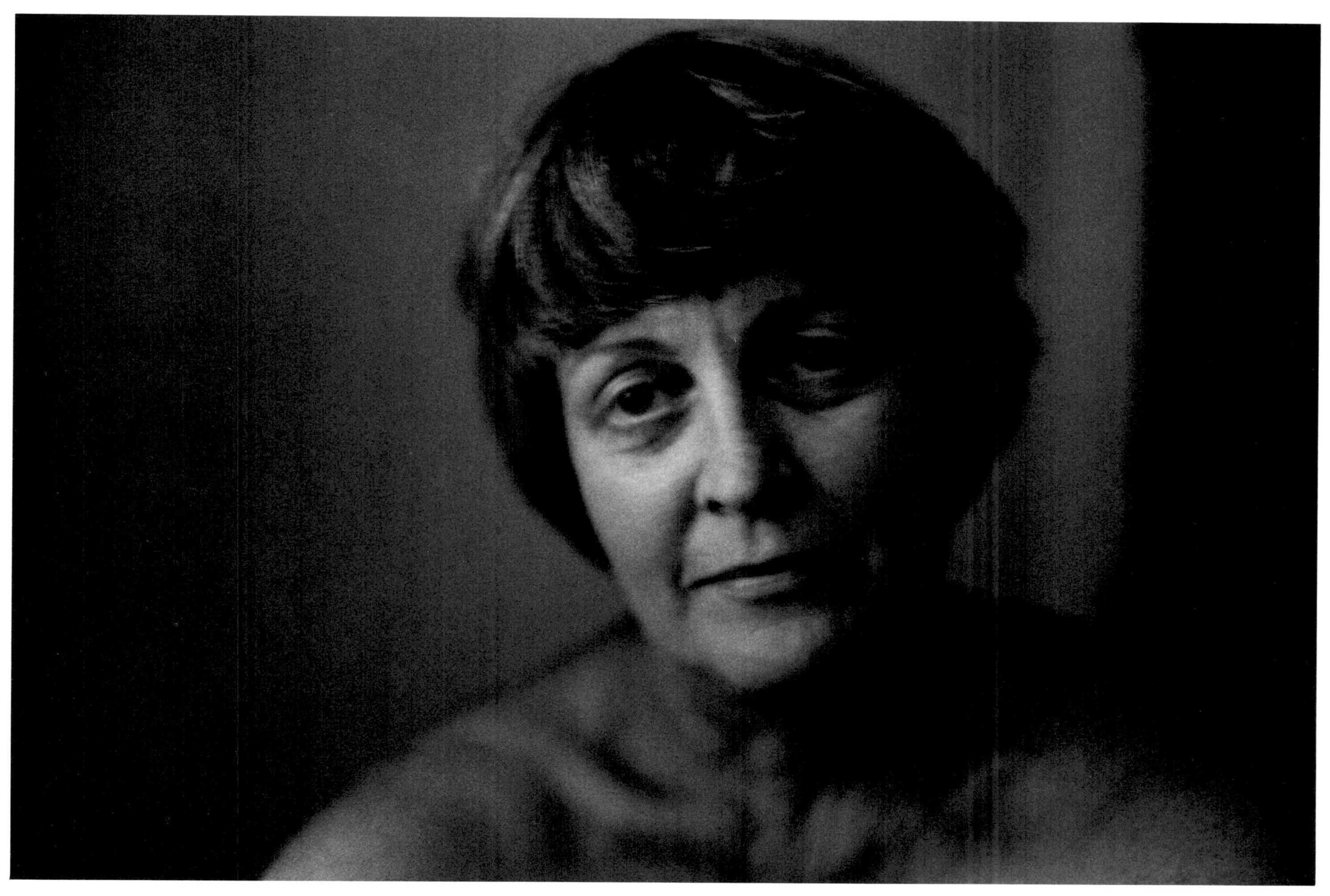

Darla Masterson, "Miss Amarillo College, 1956"   1983

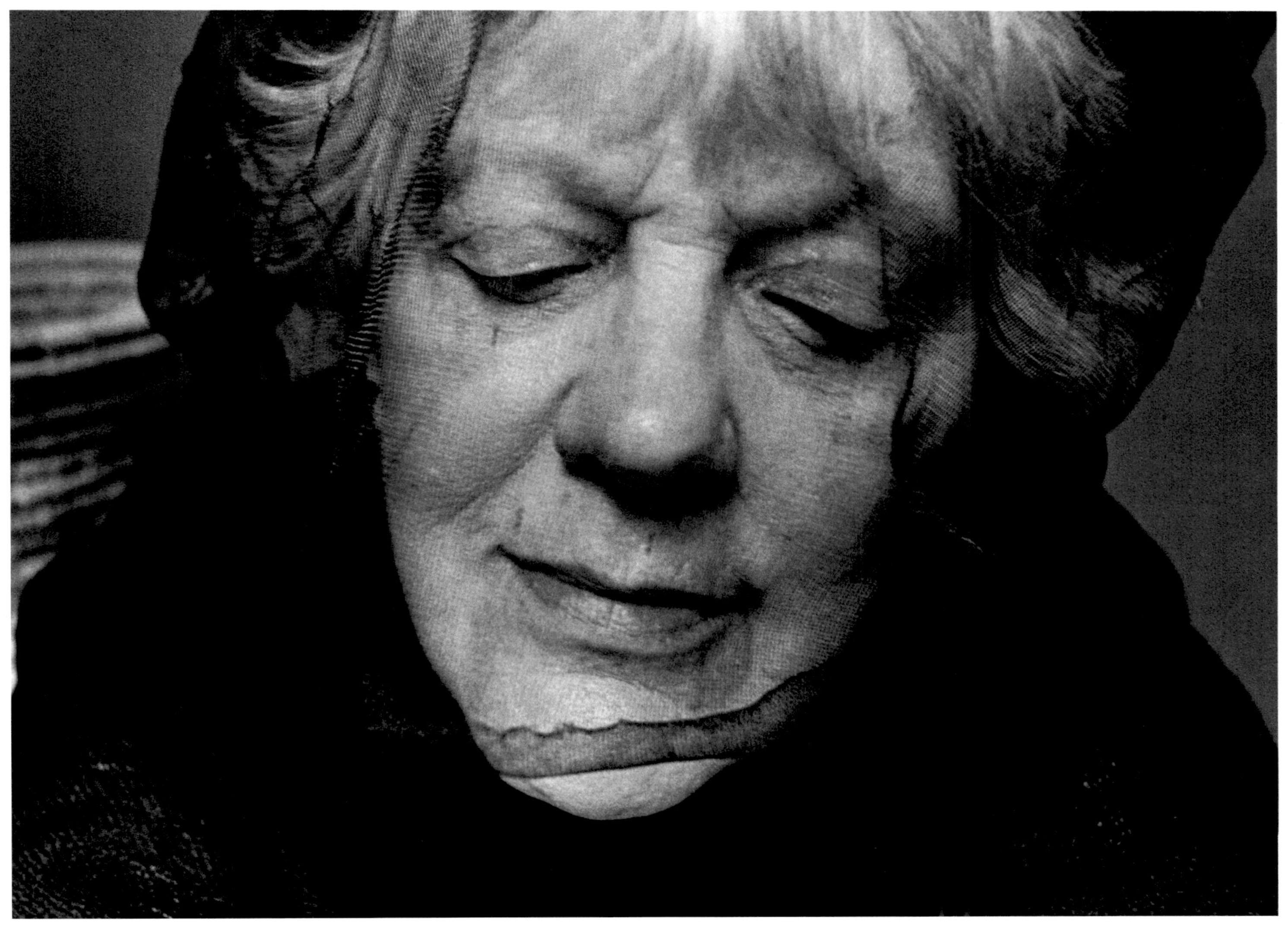

The Late Great Me   1983

Where are you tonight while the sky reflects my solitary presence.
Where are you now those of you who might whisper I love you,
are you in a watery grave down under the sea with a picture of me smiling in your hip pocket.
Where did all the promise go where did all the friends go. Have we dissolved into the past,
are we granny or auntie or that old lady down the street. I have lost my way
and my face reminds me of that. Every stop and start, love and loss legible.
A whole individual story and who will read it.
Who will look at my face and find me there?

Anne Noggle   1982

SILVER LINING

Designed by Barbara Jellow
Composed by the
University of New Mexico Printing Plant
in VIP Garamond #3
Printed by Meriden Gravure Company
on Quintessence Dull Enamel
Binding by Stinehour Press
in Holliston Roxite Linen and
stamped in dusted foil